GRANT

The Man Who Won the Civil War

Robin H. Neillands

GRANT

*The Man Who
Won the Civil War*

Robin H. Neillands

Cold Spring Press

Cold Spring Press

P.O. Box 284
Cold Spring Harbor, NY 11724
E-mail: Jopenroad@aol.com

Copyright©2004 by Robin H. Neillands
ISBN 1-59360-022-4
Library of Congress Control No. 2004104669
- All Rights Reserved -

Printed in the United States of America

CONTENTS

LIST OF MAPS

FOREWORD

When Confederate batteries fired on the Union garrison of Fort Sumter in Charleston harbour, South Carolina, in the early hours of April 12 1861, thus precipitating the American Civil War, seldom in history can two opposing sides have been so unprepared to fight a major war. The regular army of the United States was 16,000 strong when the southern states seceded, creating the Confederate States of America a few weeks before Fort Sumter was bombarded. Of the 15,000 enlisted men in that regular army, only twenty-six are known to have deserted to the Confederacy at the outbreak of war. With the officers it was very different. In 1861 there were 1,080 regular officers in service in the US Army: 620 were Northerners and 460 from the South. Some 25 per cent had been commissioned from civil life; the remaining 821 were West Pointers, and 330 of these were from the South. Just over half of these resigned to join the Confederate States Army (CSA). Of the 130 Southerners commissioned into the US Army from civil life, all but one left and joined the CSA: the one exception was General Winfield Scott, Chief of Staff of the US Army.

The Union was left with just 604 regulars to officer what eventually became sixteen armies totalling over two million men. Ex- regular officers, especially West Pointers, were at a premium, and one of them was Ulysses Simpson Grant. Except as a brilliant horseman, Grant did not distinguish himself at West Point. He finished the Mexican War with two citations for gallantry and one for meritorious conduct. In 1854, bored with peacetime service and missing his wife and children, he resigned from the Army and settled in Missouri at the home of his wife. It was at this time that he acquired a name for drinking to excess – a reputation which his enemies employed in an effort to denigrate him from time to time throughout the Civil War. As Robin Neillands points out, Grant probably drank no more than any other officer in what was then a hard-drinking army, and considerably less than some.

Grant's business ventures in civil life all failed, and when Lincoln called for volunteers in 1861, he offered his services. Political influence – seen at the time as a healthy symptom of democracy but now as undue meddling by politicians – was to be the bane of the armies on both sides almost until the end of the war. Appointments at all levels in the Union (and Confederate) Armies were in the gift of politicians, both national and state, often despite the worth, or otherwise, of the recipients. Regiments were raised by each state, and many a colonel was given command because of whom, rather than what, he knew. Woe betide an aspiring candidate for appointment in the Army if he did not have the right connections, or had offended an influential politician.

For lack of such influence, the Wisconsin lawyer Frank Haskell remained a lieutenant on the staff of the Union Second Corps for two years, despite recommendations for promotion by Meade, the army commander, including special mention for bravery at Gettysburg. Haskell was elevated to regimental command only when a family friend was elected Governor of Wisconsin in 1864. The appointment of the young Robert Gould Shaw to command the 54th Massachusetts Coloured

Infantry had everything to do with his father, the prominent Boston slavery abolitionist, and his influence with the state governor, and nothing to do with Shaw's qualification for command, which was minimal. Ben Butler, the lawyer and northern politician, became a major-general on the outbreak of war, eventually becoming an army commander under Grant. Yet despite abundant evidence of his bumbling over three years, only in 1864, after re-election, did Lincoln dare relieve him of command, although Grant had been reporting on him adversely for months.

One should not, however, assume that gifted amateurs were lacking. Among the most notable on the Union side was university professor Joshua Lawrence Chamberlain, who was awarded the Congressional Medal of Honour as CO of the 20th Maine for the epic defence of the Little Round Top at Gettysburg, and subsequently commanded a brigade and, briefly, a division. On the Confederate side, Nathan Bedford Forrest, who rose from private to lieutenant general, and the lawyer John B. Gordon, who was promoted from volunteer captain to brigadier general within a year and became a divisional commander in Lee's Army of Northern Virginia, were as good soldiers as any regular, and better than most.

In 1861, Grant was appointed brigadier general at the instigation of Congressman Washburne. Here was an example of political influence working to the Army's advantage, by helping able officers to secure appointments which enabled them to climb the career tree and to reach positions where they could have a real effect on the conduct of the war far more rapidly than they could have done had such influence not been applied. So it was with Grant, who within three years of the outbreak of war was made General in Chief of the Armies of the United States and took over the strategic direction of the war. He may have been given a 'leg up' by a politician, but Grant's subsequent swift rise owed everything to his ability as a soldier.

He is sometimes tagged as the first of the 'moderns', and coupled with this is his reputation as an 'attrition' general, or by extrapolation, not a practitioner of manoeuvre warfare, one of the vogue military cries at the present time. Not to be an exponent of manoeuvre is to be a dull dog indeed, or worse a butcher whose only recourse when faced with a military problem is to throw men at it. This is to misunderstand Grant and, dare one say it, manoeuvre warfare. Grant's operations during the Vicksburg and Tennessee campaigns were models of manoeuvre warfare. His advance on Jackson during the siege of Vicksburg, when he deliberately cut himself off from his line of supply, was bold and manoeuvre warfare at its best. Similarly, he nearly outmanoeuvred Lee and those masters of manoeuvre war, the Army of Northern Virginia, from the Wilderness to Petersburg.

There is a school of military thought that preaches that battles and indeed wars can be won by manoeuvre alone: that by racing round the countryside one will dazzle the enemy into defeat – Liddell-Hart taken to his most extreme. These theories ignore the fact that however skilled a general may be at manoeuvre, if he is up against an equally skilled opponent – Robert E. Lee, say – then to defeat him, the 'rubber eventually has to hit the road', to quote the distinguished military historian Richard Holmes when speaking to the British Joint Services Command and Staff College. In other words, canny manoeuvre may get you into an advantageous situation, but against a determined, well-led army that is not inclined to throw in the towel without a scrap, indeed may fight hard even if eventual defeat stares it in the face – as did the Army of Northern Virginia or, in a more modern context, the German army in the First or Second World War – you can expect to take very large numbers of casualties once contact is made. Manoeuvre as he might, it took Grant ten months to break the siege of Petersburg, which was not a siege in the purest sense because the town was not ringed by Union works, and consequently the Confederates were able to bring in supplies and reinforcements up to the end. The 'siege', which in the end involved a Union trench system stretching for fifty miles, was a foretaste of the problems facing both sides on the Western Front in the First World War exactly fifty years later. It was an example that went unheeded.

Grant was a very great general. He could both manoeuvre and slug it out. He had physical and moral courage, and abundant common sense. He was a good picker of subordinates – when the politicians allowed – and he stood by those subordinates. He obeyed that key principle of war: the importance of selecting the right aim or object, and maintaining it through thick and thin, whatever pressure was being exerted by foe and sometimes friend. He deserves to be remembered as a great commander.

Major-General Julian Thompson

THE LIFE OF ULYSSES S. GRANT

The life of Ulysses S. Grant presents any biographer with a problem and this problem bears down hard on those who concentrate almost exclusively on Grant's military career. Those who believe, as I do, that a general's competence arises from a combination of expertise, experience and character, are immediately confronted with the fact that until 1861 Grant was widely regarded by his professional colleagues in the United States Army as a failed officer and a falling-down drunk.

This view, if extreme and subject to considerable qualification, has some basis in fact. Grant did drink – though never to the extent alleged by his enemies – and the first thirty-nine years of his life were at best undistinguished. His military career after West Point had taken him swiftly to the Mexican War, where he had done as well, if no better, than anyone else. After that, though, it all went downhill, as a series of unhappy appointments and postings took him away from his family, into the bottle and out of the Army. This overall picture is redeemed by the fact that, here and there during these unhappy years, it is possible to detect some signs of the competence that lay beneath Grant's uninspiring facade.

All that we shall come to in time, but no historian should be discouraged by failing to understand U. S. Grant. Even William Tecumseh Sherman, who knew Grant better than most, both as a man and as a commander, said of him, 'To me he is a mystery, and I believe he is a mystery to himself.' Another officer, who served with Grant in the Army of the Tennessee, is recorded by the Civil War historian Bruce Catton as saying, 'There is no great character in history . . . whose sources of power have seemed so difficult to discover, as General Grant's.'

Perhaps part of the problem, part of the mystery, was that unlike, say, the majestic Robert E. Lee, Sam Grant never really looked like a general. The comparison may seem invidious; after all, in April 1861, Robert E. Lee had the unusual experience of being offered command of both the Union Armies and the Confederate Armies in rapid succession. Lee's reputation was established from the start – and on both sides of the line – while the quiet, self-effacing Sam Grant, allegedly too fond of the bottle, was a different kind of general entirely. Grant, it seems, was a man who had to grow on people.

But the fact is that Grant did grow on people, rising steadily in rank and public esteem until, in March 1864, he came to command all the Union Armies and devised the campaigns that led them to victory – in just eleven months. Not many officers have risen in three years from retired captain of infantry to general in chief and none have done so well at every rank in between, but from the moment Grant returned to the Army in 1861 his star was on the ascendant and, in this author's opinion, rightly so. As a general, Grant was supreme. Grant has sometimes been regarded as a master of attrition – a view based on his Wilderness campaign – but the Vicksburg campaign reveals that he was equally competent in campaigns of manoeuvre: Grant was no one-note general. Perhaps his main talent was the one spotted by that most perceptive human being, Abraham Lincoln. 'Grant,' said Lincoln to an aide, 'was the quietest little fellow you ever saw,' but he added, 'the only evidence you have that he's any place is that he makes thing git. Wherever he is, things move.'

The Civil War made Grant. Up to 1861 there was every chance that he would have been remembered by his friends as one of those pleasant, ineffectual fellows – the sort of person 'it is just too bad about', a failure in everything he touched except his marriage. Then came the war and in that he mastered every challenge. After the war, Grant fell back again; his various business ventures failed and when he became President of the United States, his term in office was undistinguished. Then, at the end of his life, Grant's star rose again. Stricken with lung cancer, and without the funds to support his family, Grant took up the pen and even as he died, he produced a two-volume edition of his wartime memoirs, a work that became an instant bestseller and enabled him to leave his much-loved wife and family with an adequate sum to live on. Grant failed in many things but he was a very great general – and a very fine man.

CHAPTER ONE

THE MAKING OF A SOLDIER
1822–1861

On the evening of March 9 1864, a small man, dressed in the well-worn uniform of a Union Army general and accompanied by a teenage boy, entered the foyer of Willard's Hotel in Washington D.C. and asked the desk clerk for a room. The clerk studied the register, allowed that the hotel did have a small room at the back and asked if the gentleman would like to sign in. Only when the clerk examined the signature did he realise that the man waiting quietly for his key was the newly appointed General in Chief of all the Union Armies, the victor of Shiloh, Vicksburg and Chattanooga, Lieutenant General Ulysses S. Grant. It then appeared that Willard's Hotel, the Residence of Presidents, had not only a room but an entire suite ready for the commanding general, whose presence was eagerly awaited later that evening at the White House a few yards up the street.

Grant's approach to the Willard's desk is typical of the man; here was a someone who expected nothing, who was surprised at his fame, a man with the knack of merging so completely into the crowd that people hardly realised he was in the room at all. In three short years Grant had risen from lieutenant colonel of Volunteers to the head of the Union Army but his approach and attitudes had not changed at all. Outward show was of no interest whatsoever to Ulysses Simpson Grant.

The Grant family had deep roots in America. Their connection with the New World dated back to Matthew Grant, who had arrived in Massachusetts in 1630 as part of the Puritan flight from the Armenian doctrines in religion propagated by Charles I and Archbishop Laud. Ulysses's great-grandfather had fought in the French and Indian War and his grandfather, Captain Noah Grant, had fought with Washington in the Revolution. These were wars of necessity, for the Grants were not professional soldiers and Ulysses's father, Jesse Grant, declined to serve in the War of 1812, when the Americans again fought the British.

Jesse Grant was a tanner by trade and in spite of periodic ups and downs, a mildly prosperous one. He was also a man of strong convictions, in particular a detestation of slavery. This belief prevented Jesse living in the South and was one he shared with Owen Brown of Kentucky, the man who taught him the craft of tanning hides. Owen's son was that John Brown 'whose body lies a-mouldering in the grave' – an abolitionist who was to take a more direct part in the anti-slavery movement later in the century. Jesse moved about in his youth, from Connecticut to Ohio, then to Kentucky and then back to Ohio where, in June 1821, he married a farmer's daughter, Hannah Simpson. Their first child, a sturdy boy, was born at Point Pleasant, Clermont County, Ohio, on April 27 1822, and named Hiram Ulysses, the Hiram because his maternal grandfather liked the name and Ulysses after the Greek warrior who captured Troy with the aid of a wooden horse.

Ulysses's childhood was happy, for the family were prosperous and his parents kind. In 1823 his father opened his own tannery in nearby Georgetown, while a younger brother, Samuel Simpson, arrived in 1825 and a sister, Clara, in 1838. Ulysses went to school at the age of five, by which time one skill had already revealed itself. Young Grant had a way with horses and was already in the habit of riding draft-horses down to the river at the end of the working day, standing upright on their broad backs, holding on with the reins. By the age of nine, Jesse was able to remark that his eldest son had 'a wonderful faculty for breaking horses to pace', and the local farmers got into the habit of bringing their colts for Ulysses's attention.

Grant's schooldays were undistinguished for, as he himself was to recall, he was 'not studious by habit' and one of his teachers recorded later that Grant had 'no taste for grammar, geography or spelling'. Grant did display a talent for mathematics but not, strangely, one for music or composition, which so often accompanies an ability with figures. Grant may even have been tone-deaf; in later life one of his best-remembered remarks was that 'I only know two tunes; one of them is "Yankee Doodle" and the other one isn't.'

By his early teens, Grant appears to have been a small yet sturdy boy, not greatly interested in schooling but a hard and willing worker. He was not aggressive or very talkative although he seems to have been kindly and was well liked by his schoolmates. The Grant family was still growing; Virginia was born in 1832 and Orvil in 1835. Simpson, the second son, was already working when not in school and in the summer of 1836 Jesse was already planning to enrol Ulysses, who was now fourteen, at the United States Military Academy, West Point.

This was not necessarily a step towards a military career. West Point offered a sound education to able young men with all the expenses borne by the US Government, a considerable inducement to families with small means and clever children. Jesse believed his eldest son to be bright but putting him down for West Point was seen in the family as an educational opportunity rather than a career move. To prepare his son for the entry examinations, Jesse sent Ulysses to an academy in Maysville, Kentucky, where he stayed a year before a slump in business forced Jesse to bring the boy home and enrol him in the village school. It was now 1837 and time to press forward with Ulysses's application for West Point.

Although the United States Army was small – mustering just 6,000 officers and men in the 1830s – it had plenty of work to do and a constant need for skilled manpower. This latter need arose largely because the expanding frontiers and growing economy of the United States provided men with leadership potential and man-management skills with many lucrative opportunities in civilian life. The cream of the West Point cadets went into the Corps of Engineers where the training was excellent and the scope for subsequent civilian employment exceptional, especially in America's rapidly expanding railway network. Men therefore tended to go to West Point for four years, get an education and then, after completing the one-year period of service to fulfil their Army ontract, go onto the retired list or leave the Army completely. Apart from the many reasons to leave the Army, there were few inducements to stay: pay was poor and promotion slow; opportunities for advancement were limited and service on the Western frontier was both lonely and dangerous.

Entry to West Point was therefore much sought-after. There was stiff competition for the available places but a family friend and US Congressman, Thomas Harmer, provided the necessary nomination and Ulysses was accepted. At this time his name changed somewhat. When filling in the nomination papers, Harmer forgot the Hiram and put the boy down as 'Ulysses Simpson Grant'. That was the name entered on the Academy rolls and nobody thought it worth arguing about later.

Nor was 'Ulysses' much used anyway; thanks to his initials – and the popular public reference to the USA as 'Uncle Sam' – Grant was known to his intimates as Sam.

And so, on May 29 1839, Sam Grant entered West Point as an officer cadet. At five feet one inch in height, he was just tall enough to get in, but at 117 pounds of slight build, too slight, it might seem, to endure the relentless 'hazing' to which all first-year cadets were subjected. The West Point day began at 0500hrs and ended at 2200hrs; the time between was taken up with drill, inspections, drill, lessons, drill and more drill, the academic curriculum covering ten subjects: chemistry, civil and military engineering, ethics, French, geography, history, mathematics, mineralogy, natural philosophy and tactics. The first hurdle was the entrance exam taken at the end of the first month, a combined paper covering arithmetic, reading, spelling and writing which routinely failed over half the applicants. Much to his surprise, Grant passed the exam without difficulty and was one of the sixty cadets admitted for a four-year course of study leading to a commission in the US Army. Grant himself had no great interest in following a military career. 'The military life had no charms for me,' he wrote in his memoirs, 'and I had not the faintest idea of staying in the Army even if I should be graduated, which I did not expect.'

Two men aroused Grant's admiration at this time: the Superintendent of the Academy, General Winfield Scott, known in the US Army as 'Old Fuss and Feathers', a hero of the War of 1812 and, in Grant's view, 'the finest specimen of manhood my eyes had ever beheld', and the Commandant of Cadets, Captain Charles F. Smith. To these were added, though at a distance, some of the senior year men such as William Tecumseh Sherman and Sherman's friend, George H. Thomas. Other cadets at West Point during this time included William S. Rosecrans and the Virginian, Richard 'Dick' Ewell. For 'plebes' like Grant, contact with their seniors was minimal: their main task was to avoid attracting demerits for some failure or breach of the various West Point codes: being late on parade, failing to shave, dropping a musket, missing a lecture.

At the end of his first month Grant had totted up only seven demerits – well below the class average, which was headed by a cadet who in four weeks collected the impressive total of 107. Any cadet collecting more than 200 demerits was dismissed, but while almost everyone collected a goodly number, it was pointed out to the plebes that one cadet from Virginia had survived four years at the Academy and graduated in 1829 without collecting any demerits at all. That cadet had already passed on into the Corps of Engineers, but no one at West Point was allowed to forget the example set by Robert E. Lee.

Grant's time at West Point was unremarkable. He passed the second, six-month exam easily and generally found the academic standards of the Academy well within his grasp – and the mathematics far too easy. This being so, Grant appears to have made little effort to improve his grades; he stayed in the middle of his class, noted by his instructors only for an outstanding horsemanship – another cadet recalls him as 'the most daring horseman in the Academy' – and a sound grasp of mathematics, geometry and trigonometry. Grant's aim in life at this time were was to complete his studies and then either return to West Point as an instructor in mathematics or find some similar post at a civilian college; taking up a military career or entering the family tanning business does not seem to have appealed to him.

At the end of his first year Grant stood twenty-seventh among his entry, about halfway, and there he stayed. In his second year, a number of cadets joined the Academy, officers he would serve with or against in later life, men such as Simon Bolivar Buckner, W. S. Hancock and Bernard Bee. At the end of his second year, Grant stood twenty-fourth in his class and in 1843 he graduated twenty-first in a class of thirty-nine – again, almost in the middle. This was not good enough to get him into the Corps of Engineers – only the top six could manage that.

Grant still hoped to return to West Point and teach in the mathematics department but he had first to serve a year in the Army, so he applied for a commission in either the Dragoons or the Infantry. With his skill in horsemanship, the former might have been in his gift but no Army works like that; in July 1843, twenty-one-year-old Ulysses S. Grant was commissioned into the 4th Infantry as a brevet second lieutenant on a pay of $64 a month and joined his regiment at Jefferson Barracks, St Louis, at the end of September.

He entered the Army at a fortunate hour. War was in the air with all its prospects of employment and promotion, even if this was a war of which many Americans, including Second Lieutenant Grant, strongly disapproved. The potential enemy was Mexico and the *casus belli* the territory of the newly founded Republic of Texas, which, after a brief existence as an independent State, was now seeking to amalgamate with the United States. The Government of Mexico was implacably opposed to the move because any annexation of Texas by the United States would shift the border south, from the Neuces river to the Rio Grande. Indeed, this also seemed like territorial aggression to many liberal Americans, but there was another factor: Texas was a slave state and any extension of slavery was not something the Northern liberals wanted to encourage.

The 4th Infantry Regiment was small, with just twenty-one officers and fewer than 500 men. The colonel was old and happy to stay in barracks and the regiment was run by its lieutenant colonel, John Garland. Among the other officers at St Louis were two men Grant had come to know at West Point, James Longstreet, who was also in the 4th Infantry, and Don Carlos Buell, who was in the second of the garrison regiments, the 3rd Infantry, both regiments having recently returned from service against the Sioux on the Western Plains. Grant devoted his time to his duties, to the study of mathematics and to visiting the Dents, the family of Fred Dent, his room mate at West Point. Before long, Grant was particularly smitten with one of the Dent girls, Julia. The Dents were a slave-owning family, with eighteen slaves for the house and farm, and Colonel Frederick Dent, while liking Grant, did not see eye to eye with him over the slavery issue and had no wish to see his daughter married to an impecunious Army officer. Nevertheless, before Grant's regiment left for Texas in May 1844, he and Miss Julia were engaged. Grant was now twenty-two, his fiancée eighteen, and they were not to meet again for some years.

In April 1844, the President asked the US Senate to approve the annexation of Texas, a step which took the country closer to war with Mexico. The man in charge of the Army of Observation sent into Texas was General Zachary Taylor, a veteran of 1812 and countless Indian Wars. On March 1 1845, the US Congress voted for annexation and claimed that the US–Mexico boundary would henceforward be on the Rio Grande and not, as now, on the Neuces river, some 150 miles further north. Nor was this all; President Polk also intended to take over the territories of New Mexico and California, both of which clearly belonged to Mexico, and so war became inevitable.

Before the war began, the 4th Infantry suffered its first casualty. Its old colonel, making a rare appearance on parade, gave an order and then dropped dead. His replacement was another elderly officer, Colonel William Whistler, who, apart from being sixty-five, was a drunkard. Even so, Whistler led the regiment into Texas, the 4th Infantry sailing from New Orleans to Corpus Christi, there to await events. Grant seems to have enjoyed Texas and came to the attention of General Taylor when, after he had failed to make clear what he wanted his men to do while they removed underwater obstructions from the beach at Corpus Christi, Grant jumped into the water, fully clad, and joined in the diving and digging. Seeing this, Taylor told his staff that 'I wish I had more officers like Grant, who are willing to set a personal example when required.' This deed may have contributed to the fact that on September 30 1845, Grant was promoted to full second lieutenant.

In March 1846, President Polk ordered Taylor to march to the Rio Grande. Grant had left his company duties and was attached to the regimental supply train as commissary officer, responsible for keeping the men fed. This was a task for which he did not care but one he discharged with considerable ability – while managing to see a fair amount of front line action at the same time. The march to the Rio Grande took ten days and the Army only halted when a Mexican patrol informed its commanders that any further advance would mean war and declared the American move 'an invasion'. Even so, the advance continued and on March 28 1846 the US Army halted on the banks of the Rio Grande, opposite the Mexican town of Matamoros. Two weeks later, the Mexican commander, General Ampudia, sent a message across the river, stating that unless General Taylor withdrew to the north bank of the Neuces, war would begin. The Mexican War duly began on April 26.

Grant spent most of the war as a commissary officer, but he was with the infantry at the initial battle, a sharp engagement near Matamoros on May 8. The bulk of the action on the first day came from the artillery and Grant saw just what cannon fire could do. 'A ball struck close by me,' he wrote to Julia Dent, 'killing one man instantly and knocking Captain Page's lower jaw entirely off.' The Battle of Reseca de Palma was renewed next day and ended in an American victory. Afterwards Grant wrote, 'I find I have less horror of flying bullets when among them than when in anticipation.' The Mexicans lost around 1,000 men, the US Army around one hundred. The 4th Infantry lost three officers killed and some twenty officers and men wounded but no move was yet made to cross the Rio Grande and go deeper in to Mexico.

The most notable event in the 4th Infantry at this time was the dismissal of Lieutenant Colonel Whistler for drunkenness, and in view of the allegations of drunkenness that later surrounded Sam Grant, this incident is interesting. Drunkenness seems to have been all too common in the US Army in the 1840s, even on campaign. Given there was plenty of liquor available and not a lot to do, this is hardly surprising, but Whistler was drunk most of the time and incapable of commanding his regiment. General Taylor therefore demanded his resignation, which Whistler refused to give, on the grounds that he had drunk away the family fortune and had only his pay to live on. Whistler was court-martialled and his papers sent to Washington, where President Polk refused to confirm the findings and dismiss him. This set a poor example to the officer corps, although there is no indication that Grant was drinking at this time.

The Mexican War lurched forward again in July, when it was decided to push south as far as the city of Monterey. For this advance Grant was assigned to duty as quartermaster and commissary, responsible for every aspect of logistics from food and water to fodder and tack for the horses. This was not an easy task, one offering a great deal of work and little hope of glory. Grant duly asked to return to his Company but his request was denied by his commanding officer – 'because of his observed ability, skill and persistency in the line of duty the commanding officer is confident that Lieutenant Grant will continue to serve his country in present emergencies under this assignment'. These were sweet words but the post was hard duty, and Grant was kept at it for much of his time in Mexico.

Thanks to Grant's 'persistency', his regiment ate well and suffered few shortages, and this practical experience may well have proved the foundation of Grant's later grasp of logistics. Meanwhile, his contemporaries from the Academy were seeing action and winning laurels, which is not to say that Grant was content to stay in the rear with the wagons. In the battle for Monterey in September 1847 he went forward to see what was going on and, arriving as his regiment were about to charge, went with them into action; more than a third of the 4th Infantry's officers were hit in this engagement. For a while that day Grant became adjutant of the regiment and noted later that another brigade, far better handled than his own had been by Lieutenant Colonel Garland, had got further forward with fewer casualties. Victory went to the Americans and General Ampudia, the Mexican commander, withdrew to the south.

Grant continued to serve as the commissary officer, getting into action whenever he could find it at Vera Cruz and Jalapa and Puebla, but he was relieved of this unwanted duty in April 1847 and was with his regiment when the Mexican War entered its final stage, the assault on Mexico City. The plan was to circle the city and attack from the south but even at the time, as he studied his maps, Grant was to wonder if the Army commander – now General Winfield Scott – would not have been better advised to attack from the north of the city and come in via the shrine of Guadeloupe. This route, Grant wrote to Julia, 'would have avoided all the fortifications until we reached the city gates at their weakest and most indefensible and we would have been on solid ground instead of floundering through morasses and ditches'. On the other hand, he notes in his memoirs, 'My later experience has taught me two things: first, things are seen plainer after the events have occurred; second, that the most confident critics are generally those who know the least about the matter criticised.'

The battle for Mexico City began in August 1847. It developed into a hard-fought and bloody affair which went on for weeks, with the critical assault on Chapultepec coming in the middle of September. Much of the fighting was hand-to-hand, and in it Grant was well forward. Finally the city fell and the war ended. Grant came out of it with his share of honours, including promotion to first lieutenant and a brevet captaincy, 'for gallant conduct at Chapultepec'.

Grant's first war ended on a high note and when he returned to the USA in the summer of 1848 he was able to marry Julia, her father's earlier opposition having been worn away. Life would not be easy – a first lieutenant's pay was just $1,000 a year – but they would manage and Julia went happily with her husband to their first posting at Detroit. Julia Grant was to prove the bedrock in Grant's life. This was a fact he himself willingly admitted and one of which most of his friends were well aware. When Julia was around, Grant was happy; when she was absent or he was obliged to leave her behind, he pined for her company – and in his loneliness, the bottle offered attractions. In spite of all the later rumours, it seems most unlikely that Grant was ever really a drunk; in a hard-drinking army it was necessary to drink a very great deal to earn that dubious distinction. From all the evidence it seems more likely that Grant was a man with little tolerance for liquor, a man who found it easier to say 'no' to the first glass than to the second and who became inebriated rather quickly. Yet the stories of his drinking – which were to blight his career for years – arise from events between his return from Mexico in 1848 and his resignation from the Army in June 1854.

Grant and Julia settled down at Madison Barracks in March 1849 when he was reassigned to the post of regimental quartermaster. In May 1850 Julia had their first child, Frederick, a second arriving in September 1851. This expanding family created money worries but these did not drive Grant to drink. Indeed, in December 1850 he joined a local organisation, The Sons of Temperance. Then, in 1852, came a blow. The regiment was ordered to California, where the 1849 Gold Rush had now created a pioneer society in need of protection and policing. For this posting wives with young children had to be left behind. Grant contemplated resigning from the Army, his eight-year period of enlistment having expired, but he stayed, partly because there was no place for him in the family firm, and partly because he was in line for promotion to captain. So, reluctantly, Grant sailed with his regiment for California.

In the West, Sam Grant began to drink. Loneliness and a lack of mail from Julia – communications were poor on the Western frontier – took their toll along with boredom and money worries, but his drinking at this time seems to have consisted of two or three benders a year. 'He was always open to reason,' said Henry Hodges, a brother officer, years later, 'and when spoken to on the subject would own up and promise to stop drinking, which he did.' This comment seems to indicate that Grant's drinking was already heavy, public knowledge and attracting the concern of his friends.

Grant's attempts to boost his Army pay by trading – in ice or cattle, pigs or grain, anything to ease his financial anxieties – also went awry; other officers did well in California, but Grant was no businessman and lost money faster than he made it. These reverses led to more drinking and one bout led to a dispute with a Captain George B. McClellan, who arrived with a party of engineers on a surveying project and became extremely annoyed at finding Grant drunk when he was supposed to be assisting their final preparations. In spite of this, in August 1853, Grant was promoted to captain, after ten years as a first lieutenant. He was then sent to Fort Humbolt, a lonely outpost in Northern California, where Grant drank more and more until matters came to a head;

on one pay day at Fort Humbolt, Grant appeared on parade much the worse for liquor.

Another officer, Rafe Ingalls, records this event: 'Grant, finding himself in dreary surroundings, without his family and with little to occupy him, fell into dissipated habits and was found, one day, too much under the influence of liquor to properly perform his duties. For this offence Colonel Buchanan demanded that he should resign, or stand trial. He therefore resigned his commission and returned to civilian life.' Grant was relieved of his command on May 1, sent in his papers and dated his resignation from July 31, 1854. His memoirs make no mention of Colonel Buchanan's demands; Grant states merely that, having a wife and two children, he saw no means of supporting them on Army pay. He returned to Ohio, helped on his way by a loan from a brother officer, Simon Bolivar Buckner, who found Grant penniless in New York, but thereafter nothing went well for Sam Grant.

He tried farming and he tried property trading, but all to no avail. By 1860 he was working as a clerk in his father's store at Galena, Illinois, earning a salary of $800 a year and widely regarded as a failure. This part of his history may be an exaggeration, for it appears that he was in the family firm as a full partner and well able to earn his keep. The pattern of his life may have seemed set as an ex-officer and a small-town businessman, but by 1861, when the new Republican President Abraham Lincoln was elected, the United States was moving slowing but inexorably towards war. There were many causes, but the crux of the disagreement between North and South was the slavery issue. Tension rose, South Carolina seceded from the Union, other Southern States followed and war finally came in April 1861, when Confederate troops fired on Fort Sumter, a Union fort in Charleston Harbour.

By the time war broke out Grant – or Captain Grant as he was widely known in Galena – had acquired a patron in the local Republican politi-cian Elihu B. Washburne. A US Congressman, Washburne was intrigued to find a West Point-trained officer – and a veteran of the Mexican War – among his constituents and thought he might be useful. Another good friend was John A. Rawlins, a lawyer, who regarded Captain Grant as a hero. Rawlins was to follow Grant into the Army, serve on his staff and set himself the personal task of keeping his hero off the bottle. In 1861, Army officers, retired or still serving, especially those trained at West Point and with previous war and command experience, were rarer than hen's teeth – and if rumours of Grant's drinking in the West had reached his home town, no one was inclined to worry about past failures at this critical time. Grant himself had always been convinced that the South would fight and knew that when war came, he would be unable to keep out of it. Like many people in the North, Grant thought the war would be over in ninety days, but in April 1861 he said to his brother Orvil, 'I think I ought to go into the service,' and Orvil replied, 'I think so too. I will stay home and tend to the store.'

In Galena, on April 18 1861, Congressman Washburne and lawyer Rawlins spoke out in favour of raising a company of men for the Union cause and, needing a commander, they turned to Grant. Washburne nominated Grant as chairman of the recruiting committee and captain of Volunteers, and although this nomination was greeted with acclaim, Grant, while accepting the post, still had some doubts. He had been a captain in the Regular Army – should he therefore accept a commission in the Volunteers? Besides, regular captains were now being raised to the rank of colonel or even brigadier general, and it was surely his duty to fill the highest post his abilities could command.

Grant, typically, was reluctant to push himself forward in the current unseemly scramble for commissions but he wrote to the Governor of Ohio requesting a volunteer commission in the state militia. There was no reply, so on May 24 Grant wrote to the Adjutant General of the Regular Army in Washington, listing his experience – fifteen years in the regular Army, war service in Mexico – and offering his services, declaring himself competent to command a regiment. While waiting for a reply, he received the offer of a colonelcy in the Illinois Volunteers, one promptly followed by the offer of a colonelcy in the Ohio Volunteers. Hearing nothing from Washington, Grant accepted the Illinois colonelcy, and in June 1861 he arrived at Camp Yates, Springfield, to take up his new command. After seven years in civilian life, Sam Grant, now aged thirty-nine, was back in the Army.

CHAPTER TWO

THE RIVERS AND FORT DONELSON
1861–1862

Although the issues of slavery and secession had been simmering for years, the outbreak of civil war took the US Army by surprise. The Army was still very small, just 13,124 officers and men, and the war split the officer corps; of 1,080 officers serving in April 1861, 313 opted to serve the South – and the Confederacy were quick to offer them high rank in the Southern Armies. After the fall of Fort Sumter, Lincoln issued a call for 75,000 volunteers and Jefferson Davis, the President of the Confederacy, responded with a call for 100,000. These men, all from the State militias, were called up for a period of ninety days, and when Lincoln then issued a call for 300,000 men to enlist for three years' service, any officer who was halfway competent was rapidly entrusted with command. For those with ability, promotion thereafter could be rapid, and so it was with Grant.

He took command of his regiment, the 21st Illinois, at Springfield, on June 16 1861. The regiment contained about 600 men, most of them farm boys, familiar with firearms and used to hard work. Discipline was another matter, mainly because the officers of the regiment neither had much idea how to instil it nor realised how vital it would be in battle. At the end of June the 21st Illinois was mustered into three years of Federal service and Grant was ordered to take his regiment to Quincy on the Mississippi, a hundred miles away, and prepare for an advance into Missouri. Partly to get them used to marching, partly as a way of instilling discipline, Grant elected to march the troops to Quincy and so their military education began. By mid-July the regiment was in Missouri, guarding communications, railways and bridges against Confederate raiders and local partisans. Here Grant learned another useful lesson about the burdens of command.

The local Union commander, Colonel Palmer, ordered Grant to take his regiment and dislodge a Confederate force under Colonel Thomas Harris encamped some twenty-five miles to the south, near the town of Florida. Grant duly set out on this mission but found the responsibility of command worrying.

'If someone else had been colonel and I had been lieutenant colonel, I do not think I would have felt the slightest trepidation,' he wrote in his memoirs, but 'as we approached the brow of the hill from which it was expected we could see Harris's camp and possibly his men formed up to meet us, my heart kept getting higher and higher until it felt to me as though it were in my throat.' In the event, Colonel Harris and his force had fled and their campsite was empty. 'It occurred to me,' wrote Grant, 'that Harris had been as afraid of me as I had been of him. From that event to the close of the war I never experienced trepidation upon confronting an enemy. I never forgot that he had as much reason to fear my forces as I had his. This lesson was valuable.'

Three weeks after his regiment had crossed the Missouri line, word came from Washington that Grant had been promoted. His commission from President Lincoln had arrived and he was now a brigadier general. Once again, this seems to have been due to Grant's friend in high places, Congressman Washburne, who had obtained four general officer commissions for his Illinois constituents – though only one, Grant, was a West Point-trained, professional soldier. Two of the others, John A. McClernand and Benjamin M. Prentiss, were political appointments – the chronic bane of the Union Armies – and given to men who would cause Grant a certain amount of grief in the years ahead. For the moment, though, Brigadier General Grant was happy with this promotion and with his orders to take the 21st Illinois to Ireton, sixty miles south of St Louis, and assume command of the district of South-east Missouri.

Grant's forces were lacking in arms, ammunition, cavalry and artillery, but the Confederates were in no better state. The war had come on too fast and neither side was yet ready to take the offensive, a fact recently illustrated by the debacle of First Manassas, or Bull Run, just outside Washington DC, on July 21, when neither army was well handled and the Union Army was defeated, losing 2,700 men of the 30,000 committed. The war in the East would continue to go badly, but for the next two years that was of little concern to Grant, who was mainly occupied with the campaign west of the Alleghenies.

Grant was anxious to close with the enemy and in mid-August he took three infantry regiments – the 21st, 24th and 17th Illinois – south of Ireton, challenging General William J. Hardee, the local Confederate commander, either to offer battle or to give way and let the Federals occupy the strategic town of Cairo, at the junction of the Ohio and Mississippi rivers. Grant's force was enhanced by the arrival of two more regiments from the West, the 7th Iowa and the 1st Nebraska, but before he could move four more regiments arrived, commanded by Brigadier General Benjamin M. Prentiss, one of Washburne's other appointments.

Prentiss was under the impression that Grant was his junior and he

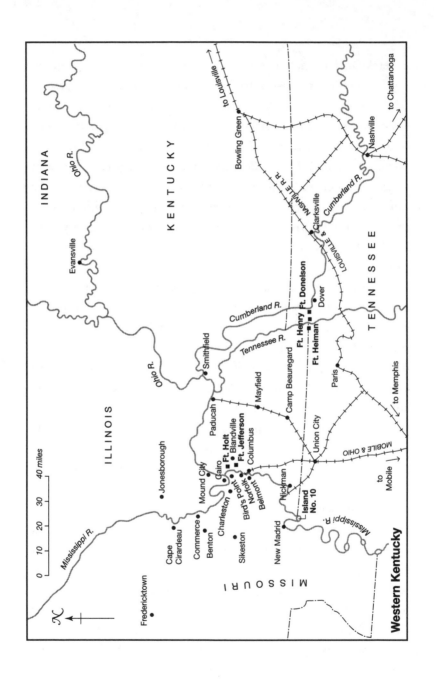

Western Kentucky

carried orders from the current commander of the Department of Missouri, Major-General John C. Frémont, a famous explorer of the Far West in pre-war years who was widely known as 'The Pathfinder', putting Prentiss in command of South-east Missouri. With this order in Prentiss's possession, Grant was without a command. This was a mistake, but even though it took little time to sort out, Prentiss still refused to accept Grant's superior rank, a consideration which Grant was entitled to as a former regular Army officer. While the argument continued, Grant was sent to Jefferson City, the state capital of Missouri, and took command of the garrison. Jefferson City contained plenty of raw recruits and precious little else – even ammunition was lacking – but this situation would not concern Grant for long. A week later he was summoned to St Louis to meet the departmental commander and was kicking his heels in Frémont's waiting room when he met an old colleague of the Mexican War, Major Justus McKinstry.

McKinstry was on his way to meet Frémont and discuss finding the right man to take a Union force into Kentucky. McKinstry told Frémont and his staff that the right man was even now sitting in the Commanding General's waiting room, Brigadier General Sam Grant. This produced the usual claims, most of them from people who had never met Grant, that the man was a notorious drunk, quite unfitted for serious employment. Fortunately, McKinstry carried the day and Frémont offered Grant the job. Appointed commander of the District of South-east Missouri, which included all of Missouri south of St Louis as well as southern Illinois, Grant was first to go to Cape Girardeau on the Mississippi and take command of the garrison. He would be joined there by other troops, including those of his previous command under Prentiss. His task was to take command of this force, clear South-east Missouri of Rebels, establish a base on the Mississippi at Cairo and, if it was considered necessary to block a Confederate advance into Kentucky, occupy the town of

Columbus on the river further south. Kentucky was still neutral in the expanding Civil War, but if the state declined to join the North, Grant was at least to prevent it joining the South.

This plan came to nothing, largely because of Prentiss, who yet again refused to accept Grant's orders and went off to St Louis to complain to Frémont. While this new argument was being resolved, the Confederate general Leonidas Polk entered Kentucky and occupied Columbus, which lay on the east bank of the Mississippi. Grant waited in Cairo – a town sinking into the Mississippi mud and alive with rats – and studied his maps. With Prentiss away in St Louis, he was now in undoubted command on this section of the Mississippi and, within limits, could decide what course to take next.

Transportation was always a major factor in the Civil War, and much depended on the existence of river and railroad facilities which both sides needed to use and were anxious to acquire or disrupt. Whatever move Grant made from Cairo would involve water transport and warships, and at Cairo he took under command a small fleet of river steamers operated by the US Navy. With these to move his troops and provide artillery cover for a landing, Grant decided to move up the Ohio and occupy the city of Paducah, Kentucky, forty-five miles away at the mouth of the Tennessee. This advance took place the next day, September 6, but the supposedly neutral town turned out to be a hotbed of Confederate loyalists and Frémont, while glad to have possession of Paducah, was annoyed that Grant had taken the town without his permission and, to underline the point, sent Brigadier General Charles F. Smith to take over command while Grant went back to Cairo.

Grant's next task was to do something about the Confederate troops under Polk. These were gradually overrunning Kentucky and it became clear that the most obvious move was to evict them from their base at Columbus. This would be difficult, for Columbus had by now been fortified and contained a large garrison. Fortunately, a frontal assault was not necessary, for just across the Mississippi from Columbus lay the hamlet of Belmont. Grant decided to strike there, for if Polk intended to send troops across the river into Missouri, he would probably land them at Belmont. On November 6 1861, Grant embarked his men in river steamers, a force of around 3,000 men in two brigades, and went down to Belmont; one of these brigades was commanded by Brigadier General John A. McClernand, a man with little military experience. Grant's transports put into the Missouri shore a little above Belmont, just out of range of the Columbus guns, the troops went ashore and began to advance south along the west bank.

The 'battle' of Belmont was little more than a skirmish in terms of duration but for this early stage of the war it involved a considerable number of troops. Seeing the Union force land, Polk sent five infantry regiments across the river to reinforce the troops already at Belmont, and when battle was joined, the two sides were evenly matched. At first, Grant's force carried all before it and the Confederates retreated, abandoning their camp and getting into considerable disarray. A Union victory seemed on hand – and then it started to go wrong. Discipline was poor and, deciding that the battle was over, the Federal troops fell out and started looting the Rebel camp. However, Polk had sent more troops over the river and, when they arrived, the Confederates stopped retreating and began to fight back. Within half an hour of an apparent Union victory, the Confederates were advancing again and Grant was in serious trouble; for a while the situation appeared so grave that some Union officers began to talk of surrender.

It never came to that, but the battle of Belmont was a close-run thing. The fighting went on into the afternoon as the Federals withdrew to their transports, leaving a quantity of wounded men behind. Around 3,000 Federals had gone into action and some 600 had become casualties, of whom 107 had been killed, and some later accounts describe this engagement as a defeat. Grant felt that this small battle had been useful; his raw troops had been 'blooded' – 'veterans could not have behaved better,' he wrote in his memoirs – and from now on they would know the difference between what was dangerous and what was merely frightening. Certainly his officers, and notably his personal staff officer John Rawlins, now had a riposte when anyone ventured to criticise Grant; their commander was a fighting general, always willing to engage the enemy – and not every Union officer was so inclined.

On November 9 1861, two days after the Belmont battle, Major-General Frémont had lost his job as commander of the Department, the first of many Union commanders to fall short of expectations. Frémont had failed to engage the enemy or check the Rebel advance into Kentucky and his departure was generally regarded as no loss. The snag was that Frémont's replacement was Major-General Henry Halleck, whose arrival brought new problems for Grant.

Halleck's relationship with Grant can best be described as complex. Halleck was considered the most intelligent soldier in the US Army – his nickname was 'Old Brains' – and at a certain level he was a competent, far-sighted soldier, apparently capable of high command. It has to be said that this opinion was by no means universal; Lincoln was to describe Halleck as little better than a 'good clerk'. The problem lay, as so often with general officers, not so much with his competence as with his character. Halleck should have concentrated on the big picture but instead he was a nit-picker, always willing to find fault, always insistent in having the last word in any argument, be he right or wrong. He was also not above being two-faced and was quite incapable of apologising for any error or confusion, even when it was clearly his fault. All in all, with Halleck on the scene, an adventurous officer such as Sam Grant, prepared to take risks in the field, would be well advised to watch his step.

The Confederates now occupied a line running west to east from Columbus on the Mississippi to Bowling Green, Kentucky. Grant was in Cairo, north of Columbus, attempting to get his district – now called the District of Cairo – into some state of preparedness, fend off accusations that he was back on the bottle, and get on with the war. Two weeks after Belmont, Grant told Halleck that Polk had no fewer than forty-seven infantry regiments at Columbus, plus a quantity of artillery, and a further 8,000 more troops at Camp Beauregard, thirty miles to the south-east. This was a formidable force and Grant would need more men to move against it. He also needed more gunboats for what was – and would remain – the semi-amphibious war in the West.

As 1862 dawned, the problem was what to do next, but as far as President Lincoln was concerned, there was one overriding priority for Halleck and the Union Armies in the West: to seize and cut the railway linking the Confederacy in Virginia and Tennessee, probably near a point in the Appalachian Mountains known as the Cumberland Gap. This was good strategy. Cutting the railroad would sever a vital east–west route for the Confederacy, and it would bring aid and comfort to the beleaguered Union supporters in East Tennessee. Yet getting to the Cumberland Gap meant crossing some of the worst territory in the USA, a barely tamed wilderness of high mountains and forest with very few roads, and this project would need the whole-hearted support of the Union commander in the Department of the Ohio, Halleck's peer and rival, Brigadier General Don Carlos Buell.

The inability of the Union generals to act together and do something decisive to defeat the Confederates was a sore trial to President Lincoln. Halleck was urging Buell to do something, Buell was insisting he could do nothing without more men; Halleck, who was better at military theory than the hard business of war, wrote to the President in January 1862, saying that the idea of making simultaneous attacks on various

Rebel strongholds was 'condemned by every military authority I have ever read' – a view that would have surprised most of the authorities in question. At the foot of the letter containing this highly contentious piece of military wisdom, the President noted wearily, 'It is exceedingly discouraging. As everywhere else, nothing can be done.'

This pessimistic view was open to dispute, for there was still Grant. Given the chance, he would do something and Halleck was about to give him that chance. On January 6 he ordered Grant to make a 'demonstration' – a threat, rather than an attack – south from Paducah towards Mayfield, Kentucky, in support of some moves by Buell. He hoped that this would lead the Rebels to think the Federals were planning attacks on either Columbus on the Mississippi or Fort Donelson on the Cumberland, two places barring any Union advance into the South down the rivers. To back up these operations, Flag Officer Foote, the naval commander on the Mississippi and a friend of Grant's, would take gunboats up to Fort Donelson and send more up the Tennessee towards Fort Henry, another position barring progress into the South.

Grant was not over-interested in the idea of a 'demonstration'; he considered that, if he went into Kentucky with a force of 20,000 men, he might as well do something constructive. Perhaps an attack down the Cumberland or the Tennessee – a strike directly into the Rebel heartland – would be a good idea. At the end of January, Grant went to St Louis to put this point to Halleck, only to get a dusty answer from his superior and have to return to Cairo, 'very much crestfallen'. He did not remain that way for long, however, writing to Halleck on January 28 that he and Foote were agreed that they could take Fort Henry. This being so, there was general delight when orders arrived from Halleck on January 30: 'You will immediately prepare to move forward to Fort Henry on the Tennessee River, taking all your available forces from Smithland, Paducah, Fort Holt, Birds Point, etc. Sufficient garrisons must be left to hold these places against an attack from Columbus.'

Plans were pressed and on February 3 Grant telegraphed Halleck that his force 'Will be off up the Tennessee at 6 o'clock. Command 23 regiments in all'. Although the river was high and the current strong, the force made good time. By February 5, Grant had his men ashore on the muddy, half-flooded banks of the Tennessee close to Fort Henry – and found Fort Henry half under water, virtually empty of troops and all but indefensible. On February 6, Foote sent four ironclad gunboats to pound Fort Henry. The commander of the fort, deciding that it would fall, evacuated as many men and guns as possible, sending them east to Fort Donelson on the Cumberland, twelve miles away across swampy ground. Fort Henry was then surrendered to Flag Officer Foote.

Other than preparing the plan and keeping to it, Grant and his Army – which was later to become the Army of the Tennessee – had little to do with the capture of Fort Henry. It fell because it was half under water and because Foote's ironclads were able to pound the visible defences with heavy guns. Grant congratulated Foote – there was no jealousy between these commanders – and sent a message to Halleck telling him that Fort Henry had fallen to the gunboats 'before the investment was complete' and adding, 'I shall take and destroy Fort Donelson on the 8th and return to Fort Henry.' This message came as a considerable surprise to Halleck, Don Carlos Buell and the current General in Chief of the Union Armies, Major-General George B. McClellan; they had other aims and it seemed to them that Brigadier General Grant was taking the bull by the horns and indicating that the next obvious move, after he had taken and destroyed Fort Donelson, must be an invasion of the South via the Tennessee and Cumberland rivers, a dual-track river highway into the Western Confederacy for Union troops and Union gunboats.

To avoid an order to break off his new advance, Grant sent a longer missive to Halleck, stating that the attack on Fort Donelson was simply an extension of what had been done at Fort Henry: having destroyed the former, he would, as stated, return to the latter. In the event, taking Fort Donelson would not be that easy. The roads from Fort Henry were poached out by rain and Foote was obliged to take his warships back to Cairo for repair. After their success at Fort Henry, it seemed that ironclad gunboats were the key to this river campaign, a campaign which Halleck now elected to endorse. On February 11 he urged Foote to get his ironclads back into service and send them up the Cumberland, where the taking of Fort Donelson – a place no one had heard of three weeks before – had become, in Halleck's words, 'a military necessity'. The note urging this action also makes it clear that Halleck attributed the capture of Fort Henry exclusively to Foote and urged him to enhance his reputation by doing the same thing at Fort Donelson – towards which Grant and his army were now making their painful way across flooded country – and trespassing on the territory of Don Carlos Buell, the Union commander in Kentucky.

Fort Donelson was a far tougher proposition than Fort Henry. It was stronger, it had more guns, and its large garrison had been reinforced by troops from Fort Henry. Grant arrived on February 12, put his two divisions, one under General Charles F. Smith, the other under Mc-Clernand, in line of battle and sent them in to attack. This was a probe and, after his men had driven the Confederate pickets back inside the fort, Grant halted them and went into bivouac. The main attack would only begin, he decided, when the gunboats arrived in support. Grant's plan was simple, a repetition of the Fort Henry assault. He would surround the Fort on the landward side and prevent retreat or reinforcement while mounting batteries to pound the land defences. Foote's vessels, when they returned, would pound the river defences, as at Fort Henry, and surrender would surely follow. But it was not to work out like that.

The first attack went in on February 13, supported by just one gunboat, the *Carondelet,* which pounded the Fort with gusto but to no apparent effect and sustained heavy damage in return. McClernand's division put in an attack, which also got nowhere, and he pulled his men back with some loss. Fortunately, there was good news to end the day; at midnight Andrew Foote and three ironclads came steaming out of the darkness and the main attack was set for the following day.

There was now another problem. The capture of Fort Henry and the investment of Fort Donelson had aroused alarm in Richmond, the Confederate capital. Orders went out to the Confederates at Bowling Green, directing Albert S. Johnston to take his Army, brush Buell aside and relieve the fort. Time was therefore of the essence; Fort Donelson must be taken, and quickly, or Grant might be taken in flank. But the attack on February 14 did not go well. The Confederate guns were well handled and Foote took his gunboats too close. Apart from damaging several of the gunboats – putting fifty-nine shells into Foote's flagship, the *St Louis,* alone – the shore batteries killed a number of sailors and wounded Foote. He was forced to withdraw, and on February 15 he told Grant that he was again obliged to take his ships back to Cairo for repair and would not be back for a couple of weeks. With Rebel intervention looming from the direction of Bowling Green, this was dire news indeed.

At a conference on Foote's flagship, Grant urged Foote to stay on and do what he could to support another attack. Foote agreed to leave the least-damaged craft but Grant returned on shore to find that, in his absence, the Confederates at Donelson had attacked McClernand's division and looked like winning a victory. This was an illusion, however, for bleak as it appeared to Grant and Foote, the situation at Fort Donelson looked much worse to the Confederates. With the river bringing in more Union troops and gunboats, they saw Fort Donelson as a trap. Having driven off the gunboats, they had decided to break out, breach the Union line and get away to fight another day. While Grant was in conference with Foote, some 10,000 Confederates under General Pillow struck McClernand's division hard. This attack was a complete surprise to McClernand and by mid-morning the Union line was crumbling, with 1,500 men lost and confusion widespread. McClernand sent for help to Grant's HQ, but Grant was absent and no one else knew what to do. Then, and in the nick of time, Grant came back from the river and took charge.

Grant was a general with a feel for battle. The noise and confusion that disturbed other commanders seem to have passed him by. In spite of the fact that the Union line was apparently teetering on the brink of collapse, he listened patiently while the divisional and brigade commanders told him what had happened. Then he looked around, summed up the situation and gave his orders: the right flank of the Union line must be restored at all costs. Fortunately, as so often happened in these violent Civil War engagements, the Confederate attack then slackened. The Rebel soldiers needed to catch their breath and refill their cartridge boxes – and the same was true of the Union side, where a certain amount of demoralisation existed. Grant knew – it was another part of his command education – that in such circumstances the side that returned to the fray first would probably win the day. He also guessed that since the Rebel attack had fallen on McClernand's force, it was possible that an attack on the Confed- erates by Smith's division might well succeed.

This then was the plan; McClernand's men must hold their line and would be reinforced by Lew Wallace's division if that could be brought up. At the same time, Smith must mount a strong attack on the Confederate line and make those forces attacking McClernand turn back in order to protect their rear. Grant also sent a note to Foote, telling him of the situation and stating that, 'If all the gunboats that can will immediately make their appearance to the enemy, it may secure us a victory. Otherwise all may be defeated.'

Grant's plan worked and it demonstrates his ability to exercise grip over his subordinates and the situation. He had summed up the options and made a decision. Every part of the Union force had a part to play and all of them played it well; McClernand held, Smith attacked, Foote's gunboats returned and the battle was resumed. The fight on February 15 went on until dusk and when night fell it was by no means clear that the battle for Fort Donelson was over. This being so, Grant was preparing to renew the action when, at around 0300hrs on February 16, a Confederate officer came into Smith's lines with a message for General Grant.

The message came from an old friend, General Simon Bolivar Buckner, the officer who had loaned Grant the money to get home on his return from the West in 1853. Buckner wanted to know what terms Grant was willing to offer for a Confederate surrender and Grant showed this message to Smith, his much-admired subordinate, and asked how he should reply? 'No terms to damned Rebels,' snorted Smith, and Grant's reply to Buckner was almost equally blunt: 'Sir. Yours of this date proposing an Armistice and appointment of Commissioners to settle terms of capitulation is just received. No terms except unconditional and immediate surrender can be accepted. I propose to move immediately upon your works. I am sir, yours respectfully, your obt. svt., U. S. Grant, Brig. Gen.'

Buckner regarded this reply as 'ungenerous and unchivalrous' but Grant's answer was professional, not personal. Buckner was obliged to accept the Union terms and from that moment Grant was his friend again; remembering Buckner's help in time of trouble, Grant offered the contents of his purse to his former friend and any enmity was soon forgotten. Other problems remained, however, for the response to

Grant's signal to Halleck, announcing victory at Fort Donelson, was strangely mixed.

'We have taken Fort Donelson,' the signal had read, 'and from 12,000 to 15,000 prisoners, including Generals Buckner and Bushrod Johnson; also 20,000 stand of arms, forty-eight pieces of artillery, seventeen heavy guns, from 2,000 to 4,000 horses and large quantities of commissary stores.' President Lincoln and the Northern public went wild with delight – a victory at last! Surely this was something to celebrate, and the Northern newspapers were quick to hail this new hero, that rare creature, a successful Union general. Yet in the senior ranks of the Army and at Halleck's headquarters the rejoicing was decidedly muted. Grant was suddenly both famous and popular, and Halleck, his colleague Buell and the current commander of the Union Armies, Major-General George B. McClellan, did not care for that at all. Plans to put Brigadier General Grant back in his place were promptly put in train.

CHAPTER THREE

THE ROAD TO SHILOH
February–April 1862

The capture of Fort Donelson had numerous beneficial effects on the Union cause. Morale soared in the North and sank in the Confederacy, while those who viewed the War as a continent-wide struggle saw in it the seeds of future strategy. This victory, if it could only be exploited, opened the way to the conquest of Tennessee and the entire Mississippi valley, and if that were done, the Confederacy would be cut in half and eventually doomed. However, to achieve any of these strategic benefits it was necessary to follow up this victory with a rapid advance south, up the Cumberland and Tennessee rivers, to keep up with the Rebel forces and, if possible, bring them to battle again.

This course of action did not appeal to Generals McClellan, Halleck and Buell, and they were in a position to put a crimp in the plans of anyone, notably Grant and C. F. Smith, who hoped to follow it. Essentially, the argument that developed was between those like McClellan, Halleck and Buell, who believed in 'position' warfare – the taking of strategic towns, transport hubs or road, rail and river routes to bring the enemy to his knees, and those, like Grant and Smith, who thought that, in the present circumstances, while the enemy was still in disorder, the way to bring him to his knees was to find him and fight him. The big difference between these two points of view lay in the matter of time. Position warfare required its advocates to brood over maps and decide, cautiously and carefully, exactly where these strategic points were, how they should be reached and what force must be assembled to take them. The essence of Grant's war was speed and persistence, the need to keep after the enemy army and give it no time to recover. Grant's view might have prevailed had not the Union triumvirate been equally keen to put this upstart brigadier general in his place.

As it was, Halleck chose this moment to take Grant to task over a number of alleged failures in command or administration, accusing Grant of permitting his men to loot at Fort Donelson and failing to keep his superior officer – Halleck – informed of events on a daily basis. The root of the problem, apart from Halleck's antipathy to Grant, lay in the fact that communications between Halleck's headquarters and Grant in the field had broken down. Grant was in fact filing reports but Halleck was not getting them – and since Halleck's orders were not reaching Grant either, Grant acted on his own authority, moving his Army down the Tennessee towards the Mississippi line and generally behaving in a combative manner of which Halleck chose to disapprove. This carping and sniping at Grant continued in the two weeks after the fall of Fort Donelson. Even while the Press and public were hailing Grant as a hero, the denigration continued, culminating in McClellan authorising Halleck to have Grant arrested for incompetence and insubordination if he thought it necessary. Halleck was not quite ready to go that far – or he may have been canny enough to realise that such an action would cause an outcry and require better reasons than he could provide – but he kept up the complaints and nagging letters until

Grant requested a Court of Enquiry – and offered his resignation.

Meanwhile, there had been developments in Washington. Lincoln had finally lost patience with McClellan, who seemed unable to get the large Union forces moving, and removed him from the overall Army command, restricting him to the Army of the Potomac. Lincoln wanted a general who would fight and he was a strong supporter of generals such as Grant who were willing to do so, and passed on his views to the Adjutant General of the Army, Lorenzo Thomas. Thomas had also got to hear of this squabble on the Tennessee. He therefore sent a cable to Halleck, detailing the various complaints that had come to his ears about Grant and ordering Halleck to report on them. In effect, Thomas was telling Halleck to put up or shut up, to either bring charges against Grant and substantiate them or let the nation's most successful general alone. In the meantime, rejecting Halleck's request that Buell, Grant and Pope all be made major-generals – and Halleck himself be given the overall command in the West – Lincoln proposed just one of these men, Grant, for promotion to major-general, a proposal the Senate promptly endorsed.

Halleck wrote a soothing letter to Grant, assuring him of his continued support. This healed the breach – at least until the years after the war, when Grant discovered that the man causing his troubles at this time was Halleck himself. Nevertheless, it was another lesson learned; Major-General Grant, restored to full duty on March 17, would be careful to file reports, keep his superiors informed – and guard his back. For his part, Halleck refrained from attacking Grant, for a while anyway, and the pause was timely, for there was work to be done. Following the fall of Fort Donelson, the Confederate commander, Albert Sidney Johnston, had fallen back, up the Cumberland river towards Clarksville and Nashville, Tennessee. Pressed out of Nashville by Grant, he had then withdrawn to Corinth, a railroad junction just across the Mississippi line, west of the Tennessee, where he could assemble a new Confederate Army to resist the next Union advance. The State of Tennessee had fallen with Fort Donelson; it was only logical that the next Union thrust would aim at the next state to the south, Mississippi, via Corinth. Halleck could see this as well as anyone, but he would not let Grant advance on Corinth until the Army had been reinforced by Buell.

The presence of a Confederate Army at Corinth was soon known to Grant, for a Union naval officer had taken his gunboat up the Tennessee as far as Pittsburg Landing and gone ashore to scout the ground towards the Mississippi line. This foray took him past a small wayside church known as Shiloh and on to the Memphis and Charleston Railroad. On his return he reported that the Confederates were massing at Corinth and would probably make their stand there. But making a stand was the last thought in the mind of the Confederate commanders in Corinth, Generals Albert Sidney Johnston and Pierre Gustave Toutant Beauregard. They knew that Buell had been ordered to bring his Army down from Nashville to join Grant's force assembling on the banks of the Tennessee at Savannah and Pittsburg Landing, and also that this massive force – some 60,000 men – would move on Corinth as soon as Buell arrived. It therefore made good sense to attack and defeat Grant before this could happen.

The recent Union disagreements and the resulting delays had given Johnston the precious gift of time to reinforce his Army. By April 1 1862, he had around 45,000 fighting men at Corinth, well-equipped and with plenty of ammunition. Grant, with a slightly smaller army, was at Pittsburg Landing twenty-five miles away with his outposts at Shiloh, and Buell, though reluctant to come south, was coming from Nashville with a force of similar size. Striking first was still Johnston's best option and on Sunday, April 6 1862, he took it, bringing on one of the most savage engagements of the war, the battle of Shiloh.

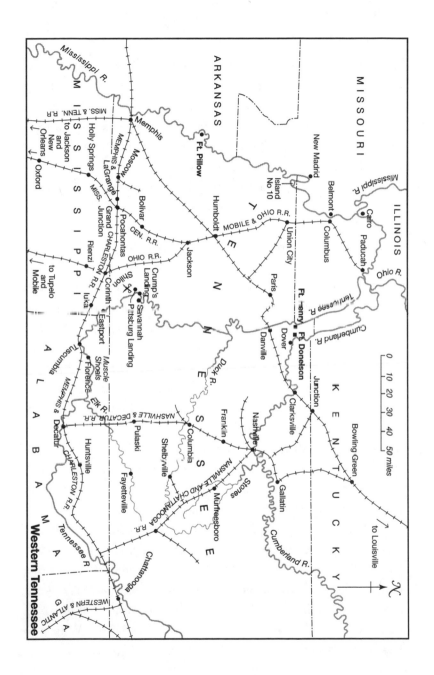

Grant had moved up to Savannah on March 5. Having established his headquarters there, he sent his divisions forward to Pittsburg Landing with C. F. Smith in command. Then Smith injured himself, a small scrape of the shinbone that seemed slight at first but became infected and eventually killed him. Grant's Army, soon to be the Army of the Tennessee, currently mustered five divisions, shortly rising to six. Four of these were seven miles upstream from Savannah at Pittsburg Landing. Sherman's and a newly formed division under Grant's former rival, Prentiss, were in forward positions, facing the Confederate outposts at Shiloh. McClernand's and Stephen A. Hurlbut's divisions were in close support some distance to the rear and Lew Wallace's division was further back still at Crump's Landing. Buell was on the march from Nashville with 40,000 veterans, and when they arrived, Grant would attack. Whatever he argued later, stating in his memoirs that 'every precaution was taken and every effort made to keep advised of all movements of the enemy', Grant clearly did not anticipate an attack at Shiloh. The Union divisions were loosely arrayed and none of them had dug trenches or erected any defensive fortifications. All thoughts were on the advance on Corinth, and reports of Confederate activity were dismissed as small cavalry patrols or picket skirmishing, Sherman bluntly assuring one regimental commander that there were 'no Rebels nearer than Corinth'.

On the afternoon of Saturday, April 5, the first columns of Buell's Army and Buell himself arrived at Savannah – and it is some indication of the strained relations between the two men that Buell did not at once report to Grant. At the same time, a packet boat arrived, bringing news from Halleck that two of Grant's divisional commanders – not the best of them, but two political generals, McClernand and Lew Wallace – had been promoted major-general. This promotion meant that they outranked everyone in Grant's Army except Grant himself and Smith, who was currently sick in bed in a room over Grant's headquarters. This being so, Grant decided that he would be well advised to move up to Pittsburg Landing on the following day and take personal charge of the forces closer to the Confederates.

He gave orders that his horses were to be ready early next morning and was having breakfast, ready to go aboard the steamer *Tigress* for the trip up-river, when the booming of heavy guns was heard from the south. This booming went on and grew louder and was soon matched by the sound of musketry. Within minutes, Grant had his staff and horses on the *Tigress* and set sail for the front, only pausing to come alongside Lew Wallace's headquarters boat at Crump's Landing and order Wallace to bring his men up to Pittsburg Landing as quickly as possible. Their destination was Shiloh, where Albert Sidney Johnston's Confederate Army had just struck the Union Army a hard, surprising and almost shattering blow.

At around 0300hrs that morning Union patrols from Prentiss's division had detected a strong Confederate force formed up for battle, close to their lines. This was reported but not believed, yet as the night wore on patrols were gradually increased until around 0500hrs, when half a battalion of the 25th Missouri went forward and got into a fire fight with the Rebels. The Missouri soldiers were supported by the 77th Ohio from Sherman's division but as this regiment went forward it ran straight into the entire Confederate Army, coming the other way. Striking with great force and considerable elan, the Rebels soon had the Union divisions in full retreat.

The full battle of Shiloh began at around 0600hrs, with a Union reverse. The Rebels struck Sherman's division and back it went, followed by Prentiss's division on its right flank. This also went reeling back, both divisions shedding men fast, until Prentiss's soldiers found some shelter in a sunken lane, where they formed a line and began to fight back. This position, which later became known as the Hornet's Nest, was held by

Prentiss and his men until the middle of the afternoon. Had they not held it with such tenacity, there is every likelihood that the Rebels would have hurled Grant's Army back into the Tennessee. Many of Grant's men fled back there anyway, towards the dubious shelter of the high bluffs above the stages at Pittsburg Landing. The shock of battle, the massive onrush of grey-clad infantry screaming the Rebel yell, the concussion of shells and the raking musketry fire were too much for many of the young Union soldiers, who had no idea the enemy were anywhere near their lines. Estimates vary on the number of Union troops who ran away; Grant later suggested 5,000 while Buell, who arrived at Pittsburg Landing later that day and was no friend of Grant, estimated the deserters at 15,000. The true figure probably lies somewhere between the two but they ran in their thousands back to the river bank and took shelter under the bluffs, refusing all orders or pleas to come out, find their rifles and get back into the fight. To this stream of deserters, which included raw recruits and commanding officers, were added a growing stream of wounded men, seeking aid or coming back to die.

When Grant himself arrived at Pittsburg Landing around 0800hrs, chaos was reigning and the terrible volume of fire told him of one rising urgency: if this rate of fire kept up, his regiments would soon run out of ammunition. Orders were sent downstream for the ammunition boats and Grant set out towards Shiloh, to view the battle and see what could be done about winning it. This was clearly not going to be easy. The fighting went on all day as the five Union divisions between the church and Pittsburg Landing were gradually pushed back and Lew Wallace's division from Crump's Landing failed to appear. Wallace had got his men on the road quickly enough, but then he got lost. His division spent most of the day wandering about north of Shiloh, trying to head for the sound of the guns and never quite doing so.

After he had sorted out the matter of ammunition supply, Grant saw that what his Army needed now was reinforcement. Johnston's men were pushing the Union Army back and if Prentiss's position fell quickly, the battle would be over and a full Union rout more than possible. Grant again sent for Wallace to bring his men forward; further orders went back to Savannah, asking General Nelson of Buell's Army to bring his division south as soon as possible. For the moment that was all Grant could do, other than try to restore order, form some kind of battle line, and find out what was going on. But communications had broken down.

When the battle began, Sherman's division was on the right of the front line with Prentiss on the left, but these two divisions were not in touch – and were equally out of touch with McClernand and Hurlbut's divisions to their rear. By around 0900hrs, Sherman and Hurlbut had been forced back, leaving Prentiss alone at the Hornet's Nest, which was now a salient, thrusting into the advancing Confederate line. This position was holding, so Grant went first to see Brigadier General William H. L. Wallace, commanding the reserve division – formerly C. F. Smith's command – which was also under attack. Pressed as W. H. L. Wallace was, one thing had to be done. On the right rear of the Hornet's Nest was a bridge over Owl Creek. This carried the road leading south from Crump's Landing, down which Lew Wallace's division would come to their aid, so some cavalry and two infantry regiments from W. H. L. Wallace's force were sent to hold that bridge at all costs; Owl Creek was flooded and the bridge was vital. That task completed, Grant sent an appeal to Buell, telling him he had been attacked by a Rebel Army of some 100,000 men – an understandable exaggeration in the circumstances – and adding that Buell's prompt response was necessary to save the day.

Hours passed, still the battle raged, and no help arrived. There was little Grant could do except wait and keep abreast of the situation. This was growing ever more grave as Rebel pressure continued to drive the

Union forces slowly but steadily back. Prentiss was the main bastion but the other one was the imperturbable Grant, ceaselessly at work behind the Union front line throughout the day, making his presence felt, calling the stragglers back, telling units holding on that help was coming, forming the remnants of regiments into small units and leading them back into the fray to fight again. Then W. H. L. Wallace was mortally wounded but his position held and somehow, it all worked. Somehow, the Union line hung on.

Much of this tenacity was due to Prentiss, who was putting up the fight of his life. He and Grant had had their disagreements but no one gave Grant better support that day than Prentiss at the Hornet's Nest. Surrounded on three sides, his men held on until around 1700hrs, pouring fire back at the onrushing enemy and killing the Confederate commander, Albert Sidney Johnston, who had rashly come forward. Even so, by late afternoon Prentiss's men were all but surrounded and out of ammunition, and when their collapse came, it came suddenly. With Rebels pouring in fire from every side and no hope of aid, Prentiss finally surrendered – a little over 2,000 men, a third of his force, were still on their feet and many of those were wounded.

The over running of the Hornet's Nest should have handed victory to the Confederates, but the Rebels had also suffered severely. Growing exhaustion, a shortage of ammunition and the death of Johnston dictated a short pause until General Beauregard was able to take over. All the commanders, Union and Confederate, were now busy rounding up any men they could find to keep the fight going and there was one of those brief battlefield interludes after which, as Grant had already noted, victory would probably go to the side that was first able to renew the struggle. As it was, the advantage went the Union way with the arrival, on the far bank of the river, of General Nelson's division from Buell's Army. Nelson's men were ferried across and when his regiments, bayonets fixed, colours displayed and bands playing, began to march towards the enemy, spirits soared; a number of those men cowering under the bluffs now picked up their rifles and went back into the fight.

Buell arrived at Pittsburg Landing in mid-afternoon. There was nothing for the generals to discuss; that thunderous initial cannonade had told Buell that Grant was in trouble and his divisions were already on their way. It is alleged that Buell, on arriving at Shiloh and seeing those thousands of deserters under the bluffs, asked Grant what arrangements he had made in case of retreat, only to be told that Grant still believed he could win. Buell's men turned the scales that day but they did not do much fighting; Grant claimed that Buell's casualties on April 6 were just two men killed and one wounded, all in the 36th Indiana, while Grant's Army had lost some 7,000 men; both figures may well be far too low but the battle was petering out and Grant could claim that his 'victory' – if victory it was – owed nothing to Buell. Buell, on the other hand, remained convinced that his arrival saved Grant from defeat.

Now, on the late Sunday afternoon, with fresh troops arriving and also a massive artillery battery of some fifty heavy guns, assembled by Colonel J. D. Webster on the riverside bluffs and about to rake the Rebel line, Grant was almost sure that victory – perhaps Pyrrhic but victory nevertheless – was in his grasp. Firing continued until dusk and Webster's guns and the river gunboats continued to blast the Confederate positions even after dark and only stopped when heavy rain came down to drench the battlefield and the thousands of wounded men lying out between the lines. Battle would be renewed next day but the Union line had held – just – and any hope of a Confederate victory at Shiloh was over. Overnight, Grant's strength increased. Lew Wallace's division finally came in and was sent into the front line to spearhead next day's attack and more of Buell's regiments came down from Savannah, on foot or by steamer, to expand Grant's forces. At dawn all these new troops and the remnants of the divisions that had fought so hard on the previous day, formed their battle line and advanced on the Rebel position; the fighting began again and went on until the afternoon.

On April 7, General Beauregard was soon in trouble and he knew it. He had, at best, 20,000 men left, all of them exhausted and low on supplies, but he also knew that there was no real point in continuing this fight. Johnston's aim had been to smash Grant before Buell arrived. Since Buell now had arrived, clearly this attempt had failed; now there was nothing left to do but fall back, disengage and fight another day. This Beauregard did, after standing Lew Wallace and the Union forces off for much of the morning. The Rebels fell back slowly and the battle petered out from around midday. Although Grant urged his divisional commanders to pursue the enemy closely, if only with cavalry, the Union Army had taken terrible punishment at Shiloh and was more than happy to let the Rebels slip away. Beauregard led them back to Corinth, and no one in the Union Army tried to stop him.

The cost of Grant's victory had been tremendous. Between them, the two armies had lost around 17,000 men – and a later count put the figure much higher, at 13,000 for the Union side and 10,000 for the Confederates. About a third of all the men engaged at Shiloh that Sunday became casualties in the worst battle fought up to that time on the North American continent. Grant records that he saw an open field so completely covered with dead that it would have been possible to walk across it in any direction stepping on dead bodies, Union and Confederate, and never need to step on the ground.

Nor were Grant's troubles over. He could and did claim Shiloh as a victory, and the first newspaper reports to appear in the North agreed with this assessment. They also depicted Grant as the man of the hour, arriving when all was in chaos to restore order to the battlefield and save the day. Then other reports appeared, painting an entirely different picture. Although some of the allegations – for example, that Prentiss and his men were caught in bed by the Confederate attack – were malicious fabrications, others had some basis in fact. The Press alleged, not without some justification, that Grant and his forces had been surprised by the enemy at Shiloh and that the terrible casualty figures had therefore been due to complacency and inefficiency among the high command – and the old story, that Grant was a drunk, surfaced yet again.

Very little of this was true. Grant was certainly not drunk, before, during or after the battle. Nevertheless, he had made one crucial mistake, maybe two. First, he had thought only of what he intended to do and nothing of what the enemy might do. In praising his Army in his memoirs, he lets slip that they fought 'without entrenchments or defensive arrangements of any sort', which jibes with his other statements that he was fully prepared for an attack and had taken the obvious precautions. Some 'obvious precautions' would have been advisable in any event for, as Grant himself points out, 'more than half the army engaged the first day was without experience or even drill as soldiers'. Later on in the war, the Union soldiers needed no orders to entrench their camps; that was one lesson they learned well at Shiloh.

Secondly, Grant had failed to take account of the aggressive spirit of the Confederate soldier, private or general. He had assumed that Johnston, last seen retreating from Fort Donelson, would not muster men as quickly as possible and come back at him. This is curious since, as his actions after taking Fort Donelson reveal, Grant was fully aware of the importance of time and what Johnston might do if allowed sufficient time to do it. Yet, while preparing to advance on Corinth from Pittsburg Landing, Grant took no precautions against the possibility of a Confederate attack – blithely assuring Halleck that there would not be one. 'The temper of the Rebel troops is such,' he wrote, 'that there is little doubt that Corinth will fall much more easily than Donelson did when we do move. All accounts agree in saying that the great mass of the rank and file are heartily tired.'

This last was probably true, but Grant was to learn that tiredness alone would not prevent the Rebels fighting the Yankees hard on every possible occasion. Grant had been too optimistic. He had relied on his own estimate of the Rebel resolve, neglecting sensible defensive preparations in favour of an offensive policy, and failing to realise that such an offensive policy was not only open to the Confederate commanders but also the one they would be obliged to adopt in the current circumstances. Grant's skills were being honed – anticipating the enemy's actions, knowing what is happening 'on the other side of the hill', is a command requisite and one Grant had yet to learn – but his actions at Shiloh were nowhere near as flawed as the Press and his detractors were suggesting in the days and weeks after the casualty figures hit the front pages. The strongest evidence for this conclusion is the reaction of General Halleck. Normally so quick to criticise Grant, Halleck later wrote to the Secretary of the Army stating, 'The impression which at one time seems to have been received by the Department that the army was surprised in the morning of the 6th is erroneous. I am satisfied from a patient and careful enquiry and investigation that all our troops were notified of the enemy's approach some time before the battle commenced.'

The victory at Shiloh was Grant's, albeit at terrible cost, largely because he would not give in at the crucial moment. This took courage and grip. Any other general might have admitted defeat, at dusk on the 6th if not before, and pulled his men back across the river to lick their wounds and fight another day. This was a process much favoured by McClellan and many other Union generals, and it was the despair of President Lincoln, who knew the Union had the men to win this war if only his generals had the wit to use them. But Grant never suffered from defeatism. Asked late on Sunday afternoon if he did not think the situation extremely grave, Grant replied, 'Oh no, they can't break our lines tonight . . . Tomorrow we shall attack them with fresh troops and drive them, of course.' An hour later he was telling his Chief of Staff, John Rawlins, 'They have been pressing us all day, John, but I think we will stop them here.' This was not bravado; his line had held and with fresh troops Grant knew the position could be held overnight and the situation reversed on the following day.

Grant claimed that there was 'no hour during the day when I doubted the eventual defeat of the enemy'. All through that night of rain and chill, when reports were coming in of the numbers killed and the cries of the wounded filled the air, Grant maintained this conviction. When General McPherson came in to report soon after dark and suggested that preparations be made for retreat, Grant retorted, 'Retreat? No! I propose to attack at dawn and whip them.'

And then, finally, Sherman came in, only a divisional commander in this battle but a man from whom Grant had no secrets.

'Well, Grant,' said Sherman, 'we've had the devil's own day today, haven't we?'

'Yes, we have,' admitted Grant. 'Lick 'em tomorrow, though.'

CHAPTER FOUR

WAITING TIME AT CORINTH 1862

Grant had learned a lot about command in the first year of war and experienced both outright victory at Fort Donelson and a narrow success – as well as a bad fright – at Shiloh. But now Halleck came down to take personal command of the Western Armies as they moved on the vital railroad junction at Corinth, the next step in the inexorable Union advance on the Mississippi valley. For this campaign, Halleck ordered a reorganisation of his forces and, perhaps coincidentally, a down-grading of General Grant. Under Halleck's new arrangements, the Army of the Tennessee would make up the right wing under Grant. Buell's Army of the Ohio would form the centre and Pope's Army of the Mississippi, fresh from capturing Island No. 10 on that river, would form the left wing. Various detached corps and cavalry brigades would form the reserve under McClernand. Then Major-General George H. Thomas was transferred to the right wing and named its commander, which, as after Fort Donelson, left Grant without a field command. With Halleck on the spot and in full charge, Grant found himself unemployed, nominally filling the post of Halleck's second-in-command, a position with virtually no duties, giving him nothing substantial to do.

Knowing what happened later, it is hard to understand why Halleck failed to employ the talents of his most successful commander and was seemingly so dismissive of Grant's tactical and strategic suggestions. Jealousy may be some part of the answer, and an uncertainty over how long Grant would stay off the bottle may be another, for the rumour mill on Grant's drunkenness was rife again after Shiloh. It might also be that Halleck was simply a poor judge of men and tended to pick those he felt were 'safe', rather than those who were clearly aggressive and imaginative. Whatever the reason, after Shiloh, Grant's star was yet again in eclipse.

This being so, it would be as well to describe some of the other, broader aspects of the war, especially the situation in the East, where the Army of the Potomac was attempting to contain the skill of General Robert E. Lee and his newly created force, the Army of Northern Virginia. The first year of the war from April 1861 had begun with Union defeat at Manassas (Bull Run) in July. Following that defeat, General George B. McClellan had been placed in command of the Army of the Potomac and charged with turning it into a trained and disciplined fighting force. In this task McClellan succeeded in all but one respect. He taught army drill and discipline, skill-at-arms and how to live in camp and field. He did everything for that Army and the soldiers loved him for it, but he somehow never managed to get it into battle. Lincoln's frustration on this point eventually led him to write a note asking that, if General McClellan did not intend to use the Army of the Potomac, perhaps the President could borrow it for a while.

McClellan was a professional officer with a good grasp of Army administration and no coward. But he took counsel of his fears and this counsel told him that the Confederate Armies were always bigger than his, always better provided with cannon and always in a good position to inflict a crushing and possibly devastating defeat on the Army of the Potomac, a defeat that would probably lead to the Union losing the war. Such apprehensions seemed to be confirmed when, in October 1861, a foray by Union troops out of Washington led to yet another humiliating defeat at Ball's Bluff. Then, in November 1861, the aged General Winfield Scott resigned his post as General in Chief of the Union Armies and McClellan replaced him.

One effect of Grant's actions at Fort Donelson and Shiloh was to cause unfavourable comments about the lack of progress or aggression shown in the East by the Army of the Potomac. In spite of constant urging from Lincoln and the War Secretary, Edwin M. Stanton, McClellan refused to move and so in March 1862 he was removed from his post as General in Chief and restricted to the command of the Army of the Potomac. This demotion had the desired effect, for McClellan started to move on Richmond – and soon ran into trouble.

His difficulties began when the Government removed an Army Corps under McDowell from his command and kept it back to defend Washington. Stanton also created a separate command in the Shenandoah Valley, calling Frémont out of retirement and placing him in command.

All was set for action, but nothing happened. The Confederate John Magruder was defending the Virginia peninsula and had his army of 15,000 men entrenched at Yorktown, where, by building lots of camp fires at night and marching his men in and out of camp in the day, he convinced McClellan that the Union forces were outnumbered. Magruder kept this up until Joe Johnston arrived with reinforcements, and although the Confederates then withdrew and McClellan followed them cautiously to the Richmond defences, once again nothing was achieved.

Nor was much achieved elsewhere. In the Shenandoah Valley in the spring of 1862, Stonewall Jackson with a corps of fewer than 10,000 men bamboozled Nathaniel P. Banks, who had close to 20,000. Then Jackson was reinforced and, in a lightning campaign, hurled back Frémont in Western Virginia and drove Banks up to the north bank of the Potomac before turning south to join Johnston at Richmond. Before he could get there, Joe Johnston had been severely wounded, so the field command was taken over by the Confederate commander, Robert E. Lee. Lee's command, the united forces of Generals Jackson and Magruder, became the famous, hard-fighting Army of Northern Virginia, which soon showed its mettle against the larger Army of George McClellan. In early July 1862, Lee took some 85,000 men and struck McClellan savagely during the Seven Days' Battles in Virginia. The Seven Days lasted from June 25 to July 1 and when the week was over McClellan was in full retreat from Richmond, having lost 15,000 men, and Washington was put in a state of alarm. Lee then set out on a truly desperate venture, an invasion of the North, and his march deep into Maryland was to culminate in one of the great battles of the Civil War at Antietam.

The Antietam campaign began in the aftermath of the Seven Days' Battles. General John Pope had been detached from Halleck's command and sent east to take charge of a new Army, 50,000-strong, which had been raised to defend Washington. Lee promptly sent Stonewall Jackson north with 25,000 men and orders to deal with Pope before Pope could link up with the demoralised McClellan. Jackson duly encountered Pope's Army at Cedar Mountain in Virginia and soon had it retreating across the Rappahannock river. There Pope clung on to the river crossings, while Stonewall Jackson awaited reinforcements before attacking again. He did not wait for long. Lee and Longstreet were now in the field and on August 30 the three Confederate generals brought Pope to battle again at Second Manassas and drove him back in disorder.

It was now that Lee set out to invade the North. McClellan marched in pursuit from Washington with as large a force as he could find, around 95,000 men, but he had no real idea where Lee was or where he was going – the Union cavalry which should have provided that information were no match for the cavalry screen put out by the Confederate Army. Then McClellan had a stroke of luck; a copy of Lee's plans fell into his hands, telling him, in full detail, how many men Lee had, where Lee was going and what he intended to do. Thus advised, McClellan set off to bring his enemy to battle.

Lee crossed the Potomac at Harper's Ferry, held the South Mountain gaps and was well into Maryland before McClellan caught up with him on Antietam Creek, near the town of Sharpsburg. The battle at Antietam – Sharpsburg to the Confederates and fought on September 17 1862 – was technically a draw and therefore a small improvement on previous engagements for the Union side in the East, but on the strategic and political front it was a Northern victory of supreme importance. Both Armies sustained terrible losses – more than 12,000 men were killed on either side – but on the night of September 18 Lee felt obliged to take his Army back across the Potomac and the invasion of the North was over, at least for 1862.

Rather more important was the fact that this engagement enabled Lincoln to claim a victory and issue his Emancipation Proclamation freeing the slaves. Hitherto the North had claimed to be fighting only to preserve the Union; now this Civil War had become a war to end slavery and such a cause would deny the Confederacy any hope of aid from the European powers. Aiding a rebellion raised on behalf of States' Rights was one thing; aiding a slave state was simply not possible. It cannot be said that the issue was so welcome or so clear-cut among the Union soldiers: dying for the Union was one thing; dying for the Negro, who was regarded even in the North as an inferior and a danger to the white man's job security and wage rates if he came north, was quite another. In the South, the Confederate government and citizens were shocked by the Emancipation Proclamation; all hope of a negotiated settlement went out of the window. This was no longer a war to preserve the Union on the one hand or for States' Rights on the other; this was a war to change the Southern way of life and free the four million black people the South held in subjection – and only defeat and unconditional surrender would do that.

After Antietam, delay and indecision again pervaded the Eastern Armies. Before long, Lincoln and Stanton were once again becoming impatient with McClellan, who was, as ever, reluctant to bring the full force of the Union Armies to bear on the South and, allegedly, out of humour with the Government over the Emancipation Proclamation. McClellan was not alone in this – changing the war's aims would cause trouble later for Lincoln.

So much for events in the East. Back near Corinth, the much-goaded General Grant was about to resign. In May 1862, Grant wrote to Halleck asking either to be relieved from duty or have his exact duties and position defined. Halleck replied that Grant had 'the position to which your rank entitles you' and that had to be enough. So the Army moved on Corinth, just nineteen miles south-west of Pittsburg Landing, but slowly and surely, entrenching every night against the possibility of another surprise attack, digging so much that the men asked if they were supposed to be tunnelling their way to Corinth.

Halleck was cautious partly because, like McClellan, he always believed himself outnumbered or that the Confederate forces were much larger than they actually were. But he was also aware that the accusations against Grant over Shiloh had not yet died down, and Halleck had no intention of letting such opprobrium fall on him. Grant mentions that this caution reached the point where Halleck's subordinates were informed – and in so many words – that they should retreat rather than fight against what Halleck believed to be superior forces. In fact, the Confederate General Beauregard had a maximum of 52,000 men at Corinth while Halleck could muster 128,000 men when he finally got to the defenders' lines. By that time the Army of the Tennessee – or right wing as it was currently called – had lost one good general officer, Major-General C. F. Smith, Grant's mentor and the former Commandant of Cadets at West Point, who died of blood poisoning on April 25. Yet it had also acquired another good one in the shape of a small, bad-tempered cavalry officer, Phil Sheridan, currently colonel of the 3rd Michigan but clearly a coming man.

The Army was still deployed in three wings or corps and as it approached Corinth, Grant suggested that if Pope on the left came round to join Sherman on the right, thereby providing a preponderance of force on one side, the Corinth defences could be quickly overcome. This suggestion was rejected by Halleck so abruptly that Grant wrote later that 'I felt that possibly I had suggested an unmilitary movement'. In these circumstances, it is hardly surprising that Grant was now pulling strings to get a posting to some other area. Members of his staff were also active on his behalf, one of them writing to Congressman Washburne in Washington, suggesting Grant for the command of Union troops on the Carolina coast. But nothing came of this and the campaign went on, and successfully, Beauregard's Confederates evacuating Corinth on May 30 and Pope marching in that afternoon.

By June, however, the Union position in the West was again in trouble. The next step – certainly the one required by Washington – was an advance on Vicksburg, a strategic point on the Mississippi, possession of which enabled the Confederates to close the river route from the West to the sea, denying Western farmers any easy route for their grain and cattle. This move was stalled by the manpower crisis – as Halleck saw it, at least – caused by the need to occupy territory in order to hold it. Having seized Confederate territory, the Union forces were obliged to deploy thousands of men in scattered detachments to discourage trouble in the towns from Confederate supporters and roving guerrillas and to prevent, or try to prevent, these Confederate raiders, regular or irregular, from destroying railroad tracks, burning bridges, attacking their outposts and generally making the occupation difficult.

This factor was a major contributor to the continued Southern resistance and the North's apparent inability to overcome the Confederate Armies. Just marching into the Confederacy was not enough, for the rebellion involved everyone who lived there. The Union had to conquer the Southern States and hold the people in check, if not in awe, and that took manpower, while the South, with no intention of taking Northern territory, could fight with fewer men. The North, however, had the manpower for both tasks. There were then 22,000,000 people in the North compared with only 9,000,000 in the Confederate States, of whom over 4,000,000 were slaves. The North had some 7,000,000 men of military age, compared with some 2,000,000 in the South. Only one city in the South, New Orleans, had a population of more than 50,000. The two societies were very different.

The South was agrarian, the North increasingly industrial, although the North could feed itself with ease. Southern agriculture was based on cash crops, cotton and tobacco; the Northern and Western farms produced wheat, dairy produce, vegetables and cattle – a balanced diet – while the South starved. On the industrial front, the North produced 97 per cent of the nation's firearms, 94 per cent of its pig iron and 90 per cent of its footwear; Southern accounts are full of stories of the men marching barefoot and it was partly a search for shoes that brought Lee's Army to Gettysburg in 1863. Nor did the Northern Armies always need to march; the Northern States contained the majority of the railroads and had an industrial population well able to maintain and expand them. With all this power available, by the end of 1862 many people in the North were beginning to wonder why this war was not yet over and victory theirs. Others, the Peace Democrats and Copperhead Southern sympathisers, were arguing that if the Southern States wanted to be independent of the Union, let them go; the price of forcing them back into the Union was proving too high. Lincoln's Emancipation Proclamation exacerbated the argument, raising the issue from a political one to a moral one – and ensuring that the war had to be fought to a conclusion.

As it was, the South could still fight the war with far fewer men while enjoying the advantage of interior lines and possessing skilful generals well able to exploit this asset. Yet there was a simple answer to the Northern dilemma: ignore the capture and possession of Southern territory, keep one supply line open by defending it heavily against guerrilla attacks, and devote all the available Union strength to the destruction of the Confederate Armies, beginning with the Confederate Army in the West, which was now commanded by Braxton Bragg – Beauregard having been sacked for failing to hold Corinth. The way to defeat the South was to defeat the South's Armies and that meant fighting them, wherever they were found.

Grant, meanwhile, had resumed his district command, returning to Memphis, as Halleck had abandoned the recently introduced wing organisation after reaching Corinth and laying siege to the city. His time had not really been wasted in recent weeks and the battle at Shiloh had been very instructive, not least in disabusing Grant of any idea that the conquest of the South would be easy. The Rebels would fight to the bitter end and therefore, he wrote later, 'I gave up the idea of saving the Union in any way but by conquest.' But the war in the East now began to abut on the campaigns in the West. Pope departed and was swiftly brought down by Lee and Jackson at Second Manassas. This led to further changes and, on July 11 1862, Halleck was called to Washington and was appointed General in Chief of all the US Armies in place of McClellan. Halleck was still adjusting to his new role when McClellan followed Lee north and scraped that narrow victory over him at Antietam.

Halleck was in his element in Washington, among the Staff and the politicians, but it is still hard to see why this officer should have been elevated to the high command. The most obvious answer is that there was no one else. McClellan had never amounted to much as a field com-mander and had put himself out of any further advancement by disputing the terms of the Emancipation Proclamation. Neither had he shown any great enthusiasm for using the Union Armies effectively when in total charge. Halleck, on the other hand, could be regarded as a senior officer who got results, and even if those results were really obtained by Grant, often in the teeth of Halleck's opposition, he was generally regarded as the right man for the job that had to be done in Washington at the end of 1862.

It soon became apparent that Halleck was no real improvement over McClellan as a supreme commander, but his translation to Washington removed him from the West and provided Grant with an opportunity. Furthermore, Halleck seems finally to have recognised that Grant was the general with something to offer. On July 16, five days after taking up his post and a day before leaving for Washington, Halleck signed an order appointing Grant commander of all the territory between the Tennessee and Mississippi. Grant's only rival in the West was Buell, whom Grant outranked; both would report directly to Halleck in Washington, but if the two men had to serve together, Grant would be in overall command.

Grant, however, could not grasp his opportunity at once. The Confederates had regained strength in recent weeks, and although the

Union forces under Grant and Buell outnumbered them in total, they were widely deployed in guard and garrison duties all over Kentucky and Tennessee. The actual number of men available for operations in the field was not sufficient to deal with the 65,000 or so that Braxton Bragg and Earl Van Dorn could muster. Grant had 63,000 men under command but the majority of these were scattered on garrison duty. The important thing was to defend the hundreds of miles of railroad and get more troops in to build up the field armies while making strenuous efforts to curb the activities of the Confederate guerrillas, who in August 1862 raided as far behind the Union front line as Clarksville on the Cumberland – which the Union garrison surrendered without firing a shot.

There were some successes elsewhere, including the capture of New Orleans and Baton Rouge in Louisiana, at the mouth of the Mississippi, but something had to be done to prosecute the war in the West, not merely fend off the Confederate raiders or wait until the Rebel Armies forced a battle. In the end, with Halleck's approval, Buell elected to move east and take Chattanooga from Bragg; it is some indication of the difficulties faced by the Union Armies when operating in territory sympathetic to the Confederacy that, after two months of marching and skirmishing, Buell had still not got there and his supply lines had been cut every night. Clearly the Confederates were up to something around Chattanooga and even if only Buell was their target, Grant would be affected. If Buell was attacked, Grant must support him – and the Confederate move against Buell duly began in mid-August.

First, Edmund Kirby Smith moved through the Cumberland Gap, chasing away the Union garrison, marching into Kentucky with some 20,000 men, a march that caused considerable alarm and despondency in both Kentucky and Washington. Then Bragg left Chattanooga, also moving north, aiming to get behind Buell, recapture Nashville and link up with Kirby Smith, who was now preparing for further mischief along the Kentucky–Tennessee line. This advance was screened by Confederate cavalry under two noted guerrilla captains, John Hunt Morgan and Nathan Bedford Forrest. The Confederate generals in Mississippi, Sterling Price and Van Dorn, were also in the field with some 30,000 men and Buell had no idea where they were heading. Cavalry were supposed to be the eyes of an Army but Bedford Forrest was unwilling to let the Union cavalry operate, attacking its patrols constantly and successfully. It was quite possible that Price and Van Dorn were aiming to engage Grant while their colleagues under Bragg combined against Buell. The Confederacy was doing what the Union had as yet failed to do; it had got all its Armies in the field and working to a single plan, so that no Union troops could be spared from one Army to support any other that got into difficulties.

Stanton and Lincoln were already displeased that Buell had failed to keep a Confederate Army out of Kentucky. In September 1862, it was even suggested that Buell should be retired and his Army of the Ohio turned over to George H. Thomas, a move Thomas rejected. Grant was also facing problems, having been obliged to send three divisions as reinforcements to his subordinate, Brigadier General William S. Rosecrans, at Corinth, where the various railroad lines running north and east had to be protected. By early September Buell was teetering on the brink of dismissal by Washington and Grant was in trouble with the roving forces of Van Dorn and Sterling Price. These forces were pushing towards Corinth, where Grant's command, the Army of the Tennessee, had shrunk to around 45,000 men: only half of these were available to defend Corinth or fight the oncoming Confederates; the rest were employed to protect the railroads. Therefore, Grant's first decision, and a typically courageous one, was to abandon the defence of the railroad between Corinth and Chattanooga and gather his forces to meet this new threat. Being Grant, his response was offensive, rather than defensive.

The situation in the West was as follows. Bragg was in Kentucky, Price was at Iuka, south-east of Corinth, attempting to slip past Grant and reach the Ohio valley, and Van Dorn was two days' march west of Corinth, threatening either that town or making a move west to Memphis; these Confederate forces could quickly combine and the task was to defeat them in detail. Grant decided to deal first with Price, sending Rosecrans against Iuka from the south and Edward Ord to attack it from the west. Their forces should have combined to attack Price but they never quite managed to do so and on September 19, suddenly realising he was in a closing trap, Price struck at Rosecrans's force, brought on a sharp engagement that lasted all day and then escaped to the south in the darkness, there to join with Van Dorn for an attack on Corinth, to which Rosecrans had returned.

Grant was now at Jackson and he was still there on October 3 when Van Dorn's attack came in on Corinth. Van Dorn had 20,000 men and Rosecrans had about the same, but Rosecrans had the advantage of some well-prepared defences and these made all the difference. The battle of Corinth lasted two days and the historian Bruce Catton was later to describe it as 'one of the sharpest battles of the war', which in terms of casualties it certainly was; the Union lost 2,500 men defending the town and the Rebels 5,000, some 25 per cent of their force, in attempting to take it. When Van Dorn drew off at dusk on October 3, the Union soldiers were too exhausted to pursue him, a fact which infuriated Grant. He believed, rightly, that allowing the enemy to get away to fight another day was no way to end a battle and that a rapid pursuit was essential, however difficult to manage. Rosecrans's failure to follow up his victory caused a considerable amount of disagreement between the two officers, who did not see eye to eye anyway, but all other efforts to catch or fight Van Dorn proved equally unsuccessful.

Grant had sent McPherson down from Jackson with fresh troops for the pursuit and other units were posted in places from which Van Dorn's beaten army could have been attacked again or captured. That was the plan but in the end nothing was done. Rosecrans took up the pursuit from Corinth too late to catch his retreating foe, and when it was clear that Van Dorn had reached the Confederate lines at Holly Springs and no more could be achieved, Grant ordered Rosecrans to return. The failure of the pursuit from Corinth caused general disappointment to officers such as Grant, Sherman and McPherson, who believed that Van Dorn's Army could have been captured if Rosecrans had shown more aggression.

Even so, the battle of Corinth had been a victory and Grant's stock duly rose. So too did that of Rosecrans, however displeased Grant might have been with his dilatory corps commander. When Buell was finally relieved of his command, Rosecrans, who had been promoted to major-general as a reward for Corinth, was appointed to succeed him, taking up this post on October 23, the very day Grant had decided to sack him as a corps commander. Two days later, Grant was appointed to command the Department of the Tennessee and, with more reinforcements arriving, was soon ready to take the field again, even though the winter rains were already falling.

The Corinth campaign did at least reveal to Washington that Grant needed more men. Halleck had arranged for reinforcements and raised Grant from commander of a Military District to command of an entire Department. The Tennessee Department was a big one, covering Western Kentucky and most of Tennessee plus as much of Mississippi as the Union forces Grant commanded could take and hold. This marked the next stage of the Union campaign in the West, for Halleck also suggested that if Grant could get hold of some gunboats, then an expedition down the Yazoo delta of the Mississippi towards Vicksburg might be considered possible. As elsewhere in the West, any campaign along the rivers would be an amphibious one.

As the autumn of 1862 came on, Grant, having established his headquarters at Memphis on the Mississippi, spent time brooding over maps and then wrote to Halleck, laying out some suggestions. As they both knew, Corinth was a railway centre, with tracks leading in all directions. Even if they were constantly cut or ripped up by Confederate raiders, they provided routes on dry ground – and food for thought. 'With small reinforcements from Memphis,' Grant wrote to Halleck on October 26, 'I think I would be able to move down the Mississippi Central railroad and cause the evacuation of Vicksburg.'

Vicksburg was the key to the great Mississippi river, the artery of the Confederacy. The Union Army held its upper reaches and the Union Navy had taken New Orleans at its mouth. Therefore, if Grant could take Vicksburg, that heavily defended town on the east bank of the river between New Orleans and Memphis, the fortress that barred the central river, he would have cut the Confederacy in two and the Union would have taken a major step towards winning the war. There was no immediate reply to this proposal from Halleck, but more troops arrived and while they were coming in, Grant had still more time to study his maps for the coming campaign on the big river.

CHAPTER FIVE

THE CAMPAIGN FOR VICKSBURG
November 1862 – July 1863

If warring nations are to have any hope of victory, their wars must be fought strategically. There must be some overall plan, some aim to which the various campaigns and battles contribute, some ambition to which the generals all subscribe. A war fought without a strategy cannot be won. Ideally, this strategy will not only lead to the defeat of the enemy forces; it will also confront the political and economic problems all belligerents face and so move the war to a conclusion.

At the end of 1862, the Union had three main field armies: the Army of the Potomac under Ambrose Burnside; the Army of the Cumberland under Rosecrans; and Grant's Army, soon to be called the Army of the Tennessee. If these armies could pool their strength and act in conjunction, the South would surely be overwhelmed. This hope was quickly shattered in December 1862 when Burnside took his Army down to the Rappahannock at Fredricksburg and launched a two-day assault against the Confederate defences. The battle of Fredricksburg was a slaughter – 'sheer murder' in the words of Bruce Catton. When the slaughter was

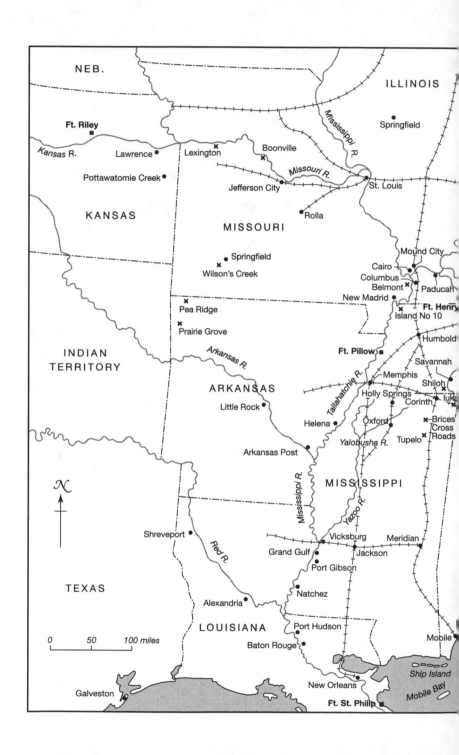

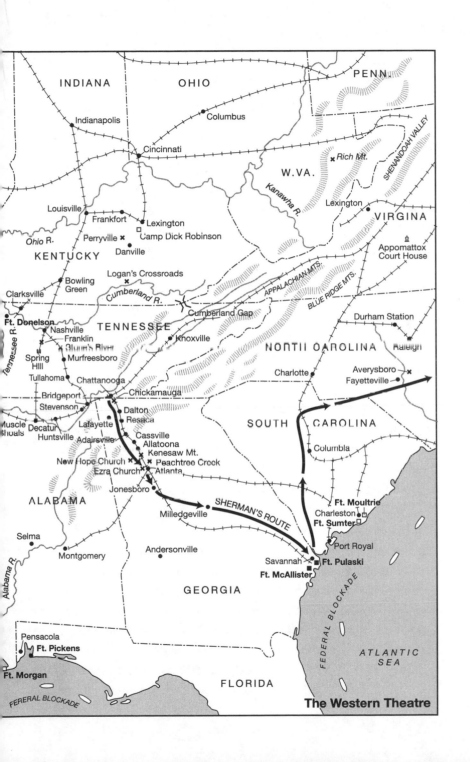

The Western Theatre

over, 12,000 Union soldiers lay stark and dead before the Confederate lines; Burnside took the remainder back across the river into camp to lick his wounds and think again. Nor did matters go much better with Rosecrans's Army in Tennessee. On December 30 Braxton Bragg brought it to a halt at Stone's River, where the Union forces were only saved from disaster by the stout resistance of 'Pap' Thomas's Corps after Rosecrans's right wing had been taken in the flank by a full Confederate division. The Army of the Cumberland held its ground at the end of the day but it could not – or would not – go forward. With two of its three thrusts swiftly blunted, the hopes of the North now rested on General Grant.

The battles of 1862 had done little towards winning the war, much to the chagrin of President Lincoln. If his commanders had any strategic plan, it involved the occupation of territory in the Southern States, a process which reduced the force they could bring to the battlefield and laid their communications open to attack. It cannot be said that any of the fighting in 1862, at Antietam or elsewhere, had done more than kill a considerable number of young American soldiers, both Union and Confederate. The war was not exactly a stalemate but it was not going anywhere either. The Confederate Armies were still in the field, and if the Union generals were to win this war, they had to do better than they had been doing up until now.

There was, however, one way of advancing the strategic struggle in a decisive way and that, of course, lay on the Mississippi. The river was the great commercial highway of the nation in the West, but even though the North held the upper river down to Memphis and the mouth of the river at New Orleans, which had been taken in May 1862, none of this restored the river trade. This frustrated the Union-supporting Western farmers, who therefore had to export their grain east along the railroads and pay heavy tariffs for the privilege. Opening the river would secure the allegiance of the West and cut the Confederacy in two, but the problem lay in the centre, between Vicksburg and Port Hudson, both of which were in Confederate hands and strongly held.

In the fall of 1862, the core of the problem lay around the swamps and bayous of the Yazoo delta protecting Vicksburg – and Vicksburg now lay in the territory of General U. S. Grant. His Army occupied all of Western Tennessee and his next logical move was to strike down the Mississippi from his headquarters in Memphis, defeat the Confederate Army of General John C. Pemberton, which was somewhere to the south, and take Vicksburg. If he could do that, and General Banks moved up from Baton Rouge to meet him, the river would be completely open again and in Union hands. The problem, however, was twofold and neither part had much to do with Pemberton's Army or indeed with Vicksburg's defences; both could be overcome if the right arrangements were made and enough force brought to bear. Grant's enemies were the Mississippi river and the swamps of the Yazoo delta. The defences of Vicksburg, though strong and well-manned, came a long way last in this list of obstacles and Pemberton's Army virtually nowhere; the essence of Grant's problem was not how to take Vicksburg, but how to get there.

There was also the matter of timing. Grant's campaign against Vicksburg was launched on November 2 1862, at the start of the winter rains, and the entire operation would be plagued by floods. The Yazoo is a meandering stream that only starts to be a river somewhere south of the Tennessee line, then loops and wanders south, east of the Mississippi, and finally drains its numerous tributaries into the Mississippi a few miles north of Vicksburg. This wide loop to the east creates a kind of moat – the Yazoo delta – fifty miles wide to the east of Vicksburg. No army equipped with the cannon necessary to besiege a city could hope to march across the Yazoo delta, so that left two other options: a frontal assault on Vicksburg's defences from the river or a flanking march to the east, via Jackson, coming in on Vicksburg along the high, dry ridge connecting Vicksburg with the rest of the state.

A direct assault on the river frontage of Vicksburg was a dangerous proposition. Vicksburg was important and therefore well- protected and strongly manned; it had stockades and entrenchments, heavy guns and good fields of fire and it occupied a commanding position with wide views over the river and the surrounding terrain. Even if Grant could get there, the taking of Vicksburg was not going to be easy – but first he had to get there. In the end, the reduction of this single river fortress was to tie up Grant's Army for the best part of six months and oblige it to undertake a great deal of hard and unproductive work. On the other hand, like every other campaign in this war, it taught Grant a great deal and contributed to that growing experience that would enable him to do so well later. There was also, as so often in this war, a political factor.

Grant began to move on Vicksburg in the fall of 1862 but he had not gone very far when he discovered that some strange moves were going on to his rear, moves that were soon seen to originate from that wily and well-connected politician – and somewhat ineffective general – John A. McClernand, who was currently one of Grant's corps commanders. McClernand had taken leave and gone off to Washington, where he had proposed to the Lincoln Administration – without consulting his commander – that he should use his political influence in Illinois and raise fresh troops for the Union cause. Having done so, he would form them into an army for the reduction of the Mississippi valley and, naturally, lead that army himself from Vicksburg to the sea.

McClernand was a staunch War Democrat, belonging to that wing of the party that supported the war and so possessed political clout. Besides, if he could raise 40,000 men in the Midwest for the Union forces, these additions would be most useful and delay any consideration of the draft by the Administration. So, while being careful not to commit themselves firmly on the eventual command set-up, Lincoln and Stanton told him to go ahead, reserving their position on what would actually happen after the volunteers came in. So McClernand went recruiting and before long fresh regiments of Midwestern volunteers were pouring into the training camps around Memphis, where Grant was waiting and very glad to see them, although more than a little concerned by rumours that another force was being created to attack Vicksburg and that his career was once again in jeopardy.

Grant need not have worried. The Administration was well aware of McClernand's military limitations – something less than a corps was about his level of competence – and had no intention of letting him take an army into the South; they only wanted his soldiers. Halleck, who knew how to draft a letter, implied as much in orders to McClernand. These directed him to send troops to Cairo or Memphis, or any other place Halleck chose, 'to the end that when a sufficient force not required by the operations of General Grant's command shall be raised', McClernand might have the command of it. No limit was set on how sufficient that force might be, but it was tacitly assumed that McClernand might then have the rest of the troops, if any, for the attack on Vicksburg. If that size of force was never actually raised, McClernand would have nothing to command.

Grant meanwhile drew up his plan for the attack on Vicksburg. His force was about 30,000 men, about the same as Pemberton's, and he would march south from the railroad junction at Le Grange, east of Memphis, down the line of the Mississippi Central Railroad, which paralleled the Yazoo but ran on dry ground some thirty miles further east. This march would be made by his existing force, the Army of the Tennessee. At the same time he would send all the newly raised troops and whatever force he could spare, plus Captain David Dixon Porter's gunboats and transports, directly down the river from Memphis – but this force would be commanded by William Tecumseh Sherman, not John McClernand. The idea was that Pemberton would have to come out to meet Grant around Jackson, Mississippi, while Sherman, reaching the Yazoo delta, would land his force at the foot of a feature called the Chickasaw Bluffs, a defended position a few miles north of Vicksburg, and take the city by storm.

By mid-December 1862, most of this was underway and almost all of it went wrong. The first man to realise that his plans were not working out was General McClernand. Having cleared Illinois of every volunteer, he cabled Halleck asking permission to go south and take up his command at Memphis. There was then some considerable humming and hawing in Washington before McClernand was informed that Grant would be in command along the river, that Grant was forming his troops into four corps and that one of these corps would be given to McClernand – which was not the original deal at all. McClernand fumed, but there was little he could do about it and Grant was already on the move. Grant intended to give the Mississippi command to Sherman, even though McClernand outranked him. Grant had no confidence in McClernand and knew, as he wrote in his memoirs, 'that by forestalling him (McClernand) I was by no means giving offence to those whose authority to command was above both him and me'.

Grant had got as far as Oxford, a strongly Confederate town on the Mississippi Central Railroad, when various disasters struck. Before advancing, he had established a big supply base for this advance at Holly Springs, some twenty miles north of Oxford, but on December 20 this vital base fell to General Earl Van Dorn, who captured the Union garrison of 1,500 men at no loss to himself and destroyed what stores he could not carry away. Without these supplies, Grant's Army would starve on their march to Vicksburg, or so it was thought at the time. Nor was this all. That relentless raider Nathan Bedford Forrest now made one of his raids across Tennessee, tearing up railway lines, burning bridges, destroying supply bases and cutting telegraph lines between Jackson, Tennessee, and Columbus, Kentucky. Grant's communications were cut off for more than a week, and when Bedford Forrest and Van Dorn rode back south, they left Grant short of supplies, virtually immobile and completely out of touch with Sherman and Halleck.

The final failure was Sherman's at Chickasaw Bluffs. Thanks to Van Dorn and Bedford Forrest, Pemberton had no reason to worry about Grant's advance and could concentrate his full attention on Sherman. Sherman got ashore and sent his men against Vicksburg on December 29 – and saw them come back again, after suffering some 2,000 casualties, all without gaining a yard. Three days later, on January 2, McClernand arrived, full of ire at Grant and fully determined to take command of Sherman's force, which, he decreed, would now be known as the Army of the Mississippi. That done, he fell in willingly with a plan put forward by Sherman and Porter and the force sailed north to the Arkansas river junction and took a Confederate fort known as the Post of Arkansas. While useful, this foray did nothing to open the Mississippi. When General Grant discovered what had happened, he ordered McClernand and Sherman to return to Milliken's Bend, a point above Vicksburg, forthwith.

The problem of Vicksburg remained the problem of getting to Vicksburg. Grant realised that his route down the Mississippi Central Railroad was too open to attack to be a viable advance and supply route. He now also realised that the river route followed by a frontal assault on Vicksburg was equally fraught with hazard, but that the obvious alternative, to go back to Memphis and start again in the spring, was politically impossible. This would be seen as a retreat and the Union – especially after that recent disaster that Lee had inflicted on Burnside and the Army of the Potomac at Fredericksburg – could not afford another retreat; the Democratic and Copperhead demands for an end to the war would have grown too strong to ignore. Whatever the snags and the risks, it appeared that the only way to get at Vicksburg was to stay south of Memphis and go directly down the river, get ashore somewhere and try another assault. Therefore, on January 30 1863, he assembled his forces at Milliken's Bend, on the river bank ten miles north of Vicksburg, and began to ponder his next move.

Grant's river campaign of 1863 is a history of endeavour – and repeated failure. Every conceivable method was tried, including an attempt to cut a canal through the bend in the river opposite Vicksburg and divert the river away from Vicksburg entirely. Had this tremendous engineering feat succeeded, it would have rendered Vicksburg a backwater, but the attempt failed when the river declined to co-operate and scour out a new channel. Then the Union soldiers tried the long approach, an attempt to get down the Yazoo delta by linking up a series of small rivers and streams east of the main river – the Tallahatchie, the Yolabusha and the Coldwater – by canals and digging a way through them into the Yazoo river somewhere near Chickasaw Bluffs. This approach looked feasible on the map and in February 1863 Grant sent 20,000 men and a number of gunboats under Commander Watson Smith to create this route. In a full month of grinding toil, Smith's force and fleet managed to get halfway to Vicksburg, as far as a Confederate position, Fort Pemberton, at the Tallahatchie–Yolabusha river junction. This fort, although ill-equipped with guns, was able to bring the Union transports under effective fire and this new advance to a complete halt. After a few days the Yolabusha–Yazoo expedition was abandoned and Grant's weary, muddy force returned to Milliken's Bend.

Meanwhile, back on the big river, Porter had been trying another approach, an attempt to skirt Vicksburg to the east by moving along the streams and bayous and putting a force ashore further south. This scheme also involved linking up a series of smaller streams and bayous – Steele's Bayou, Black Bayou, Deer Creek, the Rolling Fork river and the Sunflower river, all of which, with digging and dredging and tree-felling, might be combined into a channel to the main river. This channel could then be used to put a force ashore and supply it as it besieged the city and, in time, forced a surrender. But Porter's attempt to get up to Vicksburg this way proved far worse in every way than Smith's attempt. The entire expedition turned into a nightmare. The shallow scows and tugs went floundering through swamps, running aground, bumping into tree roots and snags, the sailors and soldiers were plagued by mosquitoes and by snakes which fell onto the decks as the vessels brushed through trees. In addition, the curses of the crews failed to drown the sound of axes as the Confederates chopped down trees to block the channels ahead and, rather more worryingly, behind. Nor was physical discomfort and hard labour the worst of it; the Confederates knew exactly what was going on and sent snipers to pick off the helmsmen and the working parties trying to clear a channel. It all went on for weeks and got nowhere. By the end of March, Grant had called this attempt off as well while another effort, to create a waterway down Lake Providence, was abandoned at the same time.

The only apparent solution, given the fact that the guns of Vicksburg commanded the main river and all attempts to outflank them via the bayous and the Yazoo had failed, was the previous option – give up, go back to Memphis and start again, following the track of the Mississippi Central Railroad and guarding every sleeper and yard of track on the way. That option was no more politically possible now than it had been some months ago – in fact, it was rather less so, in view of the obvious failure of the most recent efforts. There was also the continual problem of protecting the supply lines if this course was adopted. For the moment, therefore, Grant's Army did nothing; it stayed in its fever-haunted camps along the levee at Milliken's Bend, nursed its sick, buried a growing number of dead and tried to stay alert under the steamy rain while Grant sat in his cabin on the headquarters boat, studying the river charts and maps, thinking. Eventually, he came up with a plan.

There was nothing very clever or sophisticated about Grant's plan. Sophistication was not an element in Grant's repertoire but he had common sense in abundance and an iron will in the face of difficulty. Studying his maps, reviewing his options, he saw that there was really only one way left to force a way to Vicksburg. That was by marching his entire force down the west bank of the river – muddy roads and swamps notwithstanding – while Porter took the fleet and the transports downstream, defying the guns of Vicksburg. These two elements, Army and Navy, would then link up at the town of New Carthage and Porter's ships would ferry the troops over to the east bank. Once there, Grant's men would take what supplies they could carry and advance on Jackson, destroying Pemberton's Army if it came out to fight and then marching on Vicksburg. The troops would live on hard-tack and whatever they could gather from the country, yet this plan was, by any standards, a great logistical gamble. Grant was cutting himself off from any sources of supply; food the men might find, but ammunition would be restricted to whatever they could carry or the wagon horses haul – and the roads east of the Mississippi were not good wagon roads. Grant was moving directly into Confederate territory, where at least one untouched Army, Pemberton's, was certainly in the field, and other Confederate forces might be expected to come up if the siege of Vicksburg was unduly prolonged – always assuming Grant even got to Vicksburg.

There were two other snags. First, this sort of venture would not appeal to Halleck: it was simply too risky for that book- and desk-bound officer. Second, getting the Army down to New Carthage would be a feat in itself. There was a way, as before, down some linking bayous, but the river, which had thwarted Grant's plans with floods for the past months, was now falling and these bayous were becoming too shallow for scows loaded with cannon and a large quantity of heavy ammunition. Grant had no small boats or pontoon train and the road along the west bank of the river ran through swamps and was seamed with alligator-infested waterways. Grant, however, circumvented both these problems by exercising simplicity. He avoided any counter orders from Halleck by failing to tell the Commanding General what he had in mind until it was too late for his plans to be countermanded. The one person he consulted was Captain Porter, the sailor in command of the transports and gunboats. Porter was an independent commander, not answerable to Grant, and could refuse to co-operate. Fortunately, he was also a fighting sailor with a high regard for Grant, but although he took on the task, he issued a warning. His river gunboats and transports were stout craft but sorely underpowered. If he took them down-river, they could not quickly make their way back up again against the powerful Mississippi current – and moving slowly past the Vicksburg guns was not a viable alternative. Grant's plan was a one-shot deal. If it failed, there was no way to get the gunboats back up-river to try again. This, though, was a risk Grant was willing to take and Porter agreed to support him.

Grant got his Army down the west bank of the Mississippi to New Carthage by relying on the ingenuity and homespun skills of the Western troops in his Army. These men – farmers, loggers, small town boys – cut logs to 'corduroy' the roads, drained swamps to get the water level down, built bridges and dug canals, and whenever a horse, a wagon or a cannon sank in the mud, they plunged in after it and got it back on the road by sheer brute strength. Much has been written – and rightly – in Civil War accounts about the wonderful Army of Northern Virginia, the pride of the Confederacy, but high praise is also due for the cheery, hard-fighting, hard-working soldiers of Grant's equally remarkable Army of the Tennessee, which set out down the west bank of the Mississippi while Porter's gunboats prepared to follow them past Vicksburg.

Porter ran the Vicksburg guns on the night of April 16 1863, taking seven ironclads, all the wooden gunboats and a number of transports loaded with stores. Fuel was going to be a problem so coal barges were lashed to the sides of the gunboats – partly to provide that fuel, partly for added protection – but in the event, running the Vicksburg guns went far better than expected. Only one transport was lost and although most of the other ships were hit, it seemed that the Vicksburg guns could be passed if the night was dark and the river fast. A day later Porter had his ships at New Carthage and was already ferrying Grant's men across the river for the next step, the advance on Jackson.

Once his Army was on dry ground on the east bank, Grant's main problem was solved. Now he only had an army to fight and a fortress to take. To keep the Rebels guessing, he had Sherman make another bid at the mouth of the Yazoo, as if trying again at Chickasaw Bluffs, and in one of the great adventures of the Civil War, Colonel Ben Grierson took his cavalry brigade on a raid from Memphis, 600 miles across Confederate territory down the line of the Mississippi Central Railroad, all the way to Baton Rouge, leaving a swath of destruction in his wake. Meanwhile, Grant got two corps across the river, defeated a Confederate force and sent for Sherman to join him.

The problem now was supply, but Grant ignored it. He was now convinced that an army could sustain itself in this lush farming country and, having rounded up every wagon he could find, he loaded them with ammunition and hardtack and on May 7 set out for Jackson, sixty miles away, living off the countryside the troops passed. 'Commanders are authorised to collect all the beef cattle, corn and other necessary supplies on the line of march,' Grant ordered, 'but the wanton destruction of property, insulting citizens or searching houses is positively prohibited.'

It turned out to be a joyous march and Grant never again worried too much about supply. The route was dry and the countryside provided the soldiers with such a rich diet they were eventually glad to try a little hardtack. The enemy failed to appear, for instead of marching on Grant, Pemberton decided to defend Jackson and, when part of his force encountered the Union Army, the Federal regiments went into line and rolled right over them. Joe Johnston came up to defend Jackson but he only had 6,000 men and Sherman and McPherson took their troops into the town and drove him out. That done, the Union troops destroyed Jackson before Grant led them off to Vicksburg, driving the luckless Pemberton before him. There was another sharp engagement at Champion's Hill on May 16, after which Pemberton withdrew to Vicksburg, arriving there on May 17, with Grant hot on his heels. On that day a message arrived from Halleck, dated May 11, ordering Grant to take no chances but stay at Grand Gulf, co-operate with Banks, who was coming up from Baton Rouge, and take Port Hudson before their combined forces moved on Vicksburg. It was a little late for that and Grant tore this message up, Halleck's courier riding off, fuming. 'I saw no more of the officer who delivered this despatch,' wrote Grant, 'not even to this day.'

Grant's Army first assaulted Vicksburg on May 19. The assault was quickly beaten off, much to the disappointment and surprise of the Union soldiers, who had achieved much in the last three weeks and were anticipating a quick end to this drawn-out campaign. But Vicksburg was a strong position and the Confederates kept Grant's soldiers out of it for the next six weeks. Grant was nothing if not persistent, however, and on May 22 he sent his men in again, only to have them flung back again, losing 3,000 in the process, largely due to further incompetence on

General McClernand's part. An all-out assault was seen to be impractical, so Grant settled down to a siege, digging trenches that would totally encircle the Vicksburg defences; the Yankees might not be able to get in, but the Rebels would not be able to get out – and with Porter's gunboats on the river, there was no escape that way either.

The siege continued for weeks, with men dying every day from sniper fire or artillery. The only cheerful event at this time was the final eclipse of General McClernand. Grant had been waiting for his chance to dispose of him and in June McClernand was ill-advised enough to issue his personal congratulations to his corps, claiming the credit for the events in the current campaign – or at least the successful ones. His Order of the Day cast doubts on the fighting quality of the other corps and he compounded the insult by despatching a copy of this order to the newspapers. This sent Sherman and McPherson into a rage and the upshot was that on June 18 Grant sacked McClernand and placed Edward Ord in command of the XIII Corps.

The siege went on. The food in Vicksburg ran out, the garrison eating dogs and rats while the Yankees lived well, looting farms in the surrounding countryside, and no relief force appeared. On July 3 Pemberton sent a white flag through the lines, asking for terms. Grant toyed with the idea of demanding an unconditional surrender, as he had at Fort Donelson, but did not pursue it. Pemberton had more than 30,000 men inside Vicksburg; if these men had to be disarmed and sent off up the river to Union prison camps, the task would tie up the Union Army for weeks – and the summer campaigning season was slipping away. So, in the end, the Rebels surrendered their arms and equipment and went back to their own lines on parole, agreeing not to serve again until an equal number of Union prisoners had been returned to the Union side. In practice, this worked to the Union advantage, for many of the Rebels simply went home and declined to serve again.

While Grant was at Vicksburg, there had been events elsewhere. In early May Lee had smashed Joe Hooker and the Army of the Potomac at Chancellorsville in Virginia – though the Confederate victory cost the life of Stonewall Jackson. Then, on the day Vicksburg fell, General Meade defeated Lee at Gettysburg in Pennsylvania, and if this was another victory of the Pyrrhic variety, it was a victory none the less. Then, a week after Vicksburg fell, Port Hudson, the last Confederate bastion on the Mississippi, fell to General Banks and the river was open from Missouri to the sea. This was the logical outcome of all that Grant had been working towards since he first took up command of a Western army, and a great triumph. But there was no triumphalism. Grant had occasion to remind one officer that the defeated Confederates 'were, after all, our countrymen', and when the Rebel garrison marched out, just one cheer was raised by the Union troops, a rousing shout of praise for 'The gallant defenders of Vicksburg'.

CHAPTER SIX

THE BATTLE OF CHATTANOOGA
November 1863

With the taking of Vicksburg and the opening of the Mississippi, the end was in sight for the Confederacy – at least to anyone with vision enough to see the strategic possibilities, with the Confederacy now split in two and strong and successful Union Armies in the field. Sadly, General Halleck did not possess such vision. Instead of turning all his forces on the Confederacy, he proceeded, as before, to split the Armies up in penny packets, chasing down Confederate forces that might well have collapsed unaided.

This was doubly unfortunate because the Union was in need of successive victories – not occasional successes but some sign that this war was really going somewhere. It was now 1863, two years into the war, the death toll was growing, the supply of volunteers had all but dried up, and the newly introduced draft was universally unpopular and widely evaded. Nor was there much solidarity on the political front. Copperhead sentiment in favour of a negotiated peace was rising and the mid-term elections in 1862 had produced many candidates who were vocal against the continued prosecution of the war. In such a situation, the occasional victory, however useful and widely trumpeted in Republican newspapers, would not be sufficient to stop the growing trend towards a policy based on peace at any price. After Vicksburg, the Union forces should have moved *en masse* against the Southern Armies. Under Halleck, this was not to be.

Grant wanted to move at once on Mobile, but Halleck had other plans. He wanted Grant to occupy the territory gained and peg out claims in East Texas and East Louisiana. Grant's Army was therefore sent off in sections from Vicksburg, part of it into Arkansas and part downriver to join Banks's force for a foray into Texas, while a quantity of troops was despatched to garrison a series of forts along the Mississippi and Arkansas rivers, places under no discernible visible threat requiring the presence of front-line soldiers. After Vicksburg, Sherman declared that the Union Armies 'would be in Mobile in October and Georgia by Christmas', but Halleck thought otherwise. In his memoirs, Grant refers to the post-Vicksburg dispersions as 'the depletion of an army which had won a succession of great victories', a repetition of the pointless process of dispersion which had followed Shiloh and the taking of Corinth in 1862. Granted, he was able to pursue Rebel forces in the neighbourhood of Vicksburg and secure the town against further attack, but the real outcome of Halleck's decisions was that the Union Armies in the West were not going to achieve anything more in 1863 if this process continued.

There were some diversions, unpleasing to a fighting general and a glorious waste of time. In August, Halleck insisted that Grant should go down to New Orleans and join Banks for a victory parade. Inactivity was never good for U. S. Grant and there is more than a suspicion that he was drinking again; it is certain that this superb horseman fell off his charger at a review and had to spend some time in bed and more time on crutches before he was fit for action again. Nor was there much action on the other fronts. In the East, the great battle at Gettysburg in July 1863 had exhausted both the Army of Northern Virginia and the Army of the Potomac. They spent the late summer squaring up to each other in Virginia but never actually engaging in any effective way.

To find the action that summer, it is necessary to move to the Army of the Cumberland, 60,000-strong under General Rosecrans, which, at the end of June, 1863 left camp at Murfreesboro, Tennessee, and marched on the major town of Chattanooga on the Tennessee river, close to the Georgia line. Chattanooga, a railroad junction at the southern end of the Appalachian Mountains, was the northern entry point to the State of Georgia and in moving there Rosecrans was making a sound strategic move. Even Halleck recognised that and in mid-September Grant was directed to send all available forces to co-operate with Rosecrans in the fight for Chattanooga. But before that could happen, Rosecrans ran into serious trouble at Chickamauga.

Chattanooga confronted the Union commanders with the same problem as Vicksburg – access. It lay across some desolate mountainous country beyond the Tennessee river and the only practical route to it ran astride the Nashville and Chattanooga Railroad. The snag with this route was that Rebel guerrillas kept the railroad shut and around 45,000 first-rate Confederate troops under General Braxton Bragg lay astride the railroad at Tullahoma, twenty miles south of Murfreesboro. These two Union and Confederate Armies might have clashed within a day's march of their base but Rosecrans, in spite of Grant's doubts about his ability, was an able tactician. By shifting his advance to threaten Bragg's right flank, he levered the Confederates loose at Tullahoma. By July 4 the Confederate high command in Richmond heard that Bragg had abandoned Central Tennessee and taken his Army back to Chattanooga, with Rosecrans hot on his heels.

Rosecrans's march south was not an easy matter – nor indeed was Bragg's withdrawal – for the country was rugged, the roads were poor and the rain was relentless. Men sank to their thighs in the mud, cannon had to be hauled up mountain roads by tailing two or three horse teams onto each gun, and by the time the Union troops reached Tullahoma, both men and horses were close to exhaustion. At Tullahoma, Rosecrans heard of Grant's success at Vicksburg and decided that, since the retreating Bragg would certainly have been reinforced at Chattanooga, he would wait where he was until those troops no longer needed at Vicksburg could march south and threaten Mobile, which would oblige Bragg to evacuate Chattanooga and retreat yet again. This was a sound enough plan but Halleck could not see it; Grant was forbidden to march on Mobile and Rosecrans was ordered to continue pressing on towards Chattanooga.

Therefore, on August 16, Rosecrans's forces set out again for the south. Summer had arrived and the roads were dry so they made good progress but, even so, it took another two weeks before they came out on the banks of the Tennessee, some way west of Chattanooga. Then they discovered that Bragg had elected to abandon that city and withdraw into Georgia, apparently to await reinforcements. Rosecrans therefore sent an Army corps into Chattanooga and sent his other two corps south, urging them to cross the mountains as quickly as possible and maintain the pressure on Bragg. So far Rosecrans had done very well indeed – but on September 19 and 20, Bragg struck back at Chickamauga. His Army, reinforced by Longstreet's hard-fighting corps from the Army of Northern Virginia, smashed its way through the Army of the Cumberland and cut it in two. The situation was saved, yet again, by the stubbornness of General 'Pap' Thomas, who held up the Rebels long enough for the rest of Rosecrans's Army to retreat back to Chattanooga through the Rossville Gap and so into a trap of its own making.

Chickamauga was a fearful battle – the total casualties on both sides amounted to some 30,000 men – and when it was over, the Army of the Cumberland, severely shaken, was penned up in Chattanooga, with the surrounding heights held by Confederate troops, no way out and no viable means of supply. Unless they could be relieved or some secure means of supply devised, they had to either fight their way out or starve. In this desperate situation, Halleck and Lincoln turned again to Grant. On October 3, Grant was summoned to Cairo for a talk with Secretary Stanton, who handed Grant two orders. Both created a Military Division of the Mississippi composed of the Departments of the Ohio, Cumberland and Tennessee, and all the territory between the Alleghenies and the Mississippi north of Banks's command in the South-west. Both gave the command to Grant, who was now promoted to Major-General in the Regular Army, but the first order left the existing commanders in place, while the second replaced Rosecrans with Thomas – 'The Rock of Chickamauga' – at Chattanooga. Grant accepted the second order and, with it, responsibility for saving the Army of the Cumberland. Having sent a cable sacking Rosecrans and ordering Thomas to take charge and hold on, Grant set off for the besieged city, making his way over the mountains on a narrow, stony track, littered with the bodies of dead horses and mules. Grant's injuries from his fall in New Orleans were still painful but he pressed on and arrived in Chattanooga on the evening of October 23.

Here was the dilemma: the Army of the Cumberland could not get out and food could not get in – or so it seemed. Rosecrans's troops had gone on rations, then on half-rations, then on quarter-rations, but they had been stuck for weeks and things were looking desperate. Fortunately, some help was coming; Joe Hooker was given two corps from the Army of the Potomac and sent west to Bridgeport and the Army of the Tennessee under Sherman was coming along the Memphis and

Charleston Railroad, repairing the track as it came. But all this would take time and, with men and horses starving, time was running out in Chattanooga.

Saving the Army of the Cumberland would require some initiative but the Army itself had not been idle. Its Chief Engineer, General W. F. 'Baldy' Smith, was building a river steamer, and scouting parties had found a route over the mountains through which supplies could be brought into the city. This lay on a narrow mountain road from Brown's Ferry on the Tennessee back to Hooker's base at Bridgeport – a road soon to be christened the Cracker Line. Rosecrans had not attempted to use the route, so Grant ordered immediate action to open it and within five days of Grant's arrival, the Cracker Line was opened and kept open by Hooker's troops. Supplies began to flow into Chattanooga and, with the immediate problem solved, Grant began to brood on new ways to prosecute the war. He began by reorganising the Army of the Cumberland, reducing it from four corps to two, sacking two of the least useful corps commanders and building up the remaining corps.

It might have been possible to use the Cracker Line and the river to evacuate the Union troops from Chattanooga, but that was not Grant's way. Besides, to do that meant abandoning much equipment and most of the artillery. To Grant's mind, the way out led south, through the Confederate Army and over Lookout Mountain and Missionary Ridge, and he had to take this route quickly for there was now another problem requiring his attention. Further to the north-east, deeper in the Appalachians, General Burnside and the Union forces at Knoxville were now hemmed in by Confederate forces – and the only troops available to break the siege of Knoxville, south-west of the Cumberland Gap, were the Union forces currently besieged at Chattanooga.

Burnside had marched his men south from Kentucky, losing most of their draught animals in the mountains. His troops arrived in Knoxville having used up their rations and abandoned a great deal of equipment. Food was not a problem here for the local people were loyal to the Union and brought in plenty of provisions, but military supplies were unobtainable and soon in short supply; now under siege, Burnside had soon to be relieved or his troops would run out of ammunition. Burnside's problem increased on November 4, when Bragg elected to send Longstreet's corps – some 20,000 men – up to Knoxville, with orders to take the place quickly and capture Burnside's Army. This move deprived Bragg's forces of some of their finest troops and was later described by Grant as one of several grave mistakes made by Bragg. But detaching Longstreet's strong corps did not bother Bragg at all; he had the commanding heights at Chattanooga and plenty of artillery. With his men well dug in on good ground, Bragg considered his position almost impregnable. He was wrong.

Grant began to assemble his forces to lift the sieges of Chattanooga and Knoxville. Sherman was ordered to Stevenson, south of Bridgeport, to back up Hooker, and to solve the problem caused by moving more troops into an area without reliable means of supply, General G. M. Dodge of Sherman's command was ordered to repair and reopen the Decatur to Nashville Railroad. Dodge was an experienced railroad engineer and his men displayed that Western aptitude for turning their hands to anything by duly constructing a railroad. Trees were felled, saw mills requisitioned, blacksmiths' shops commandeered – there was no shortage of lumberjacks, blacksmiths or carpenters – and within forty days Dodge had the railroad open again and supplies from Nashville were flowing south to feed the Federal troops. However, Longstreet's departure for Knoxville caused concern in Washington and on November 7 Grant was obliged to order an attack on the Confederate lines at Chattanooga in the hope of forcing Longstreet back.

Grant ordered Thomas to attack Bragg's right, but Thomas could not attack at this time; he had no horses to move his artillery and Grant's attack had to wait until the arrival of Sherman's Army of the Tennessee. Fortunately, Longstreet only had a railroad as far as Loudon, and after that his corps had to use a narrow wagon road to Knoxville. So while he assembled wagons for his supply train, Longstreet was obliged to stay in Loudon, and he stayed there until November 13. On the following day Sherman reached Bridgeport and the first of his troops came into Chattanooga on November 20. However, this delay in starting the attack at Chattanooga alarmed Lincoln and Halleck, who continued to remind Grant of the problems facing Burnside at Knoxville.

Grant's force at Chattanooga consisted of two Armies, the Army of the Cumberland and the Army of the Tennessee, plus two corps from the Army of the Potomac under Hooker. It was more than capable of rounding up Bragg's now depleted force but Bragg had the advantage of the ground and could fight on the defensive, two factors which greatly negated Union superiority. There was also a certain amount of dissension in the Union camp. Hooker's and Sherman's men believed that they had 'rescued' the Army of the Cumberland from a sticky fate. Their soldiers did not bother to conceal this fact and Thomas's men were greatly relieved when the armies were ordered to open the attack and break the siege of Chattanooga – and give the Cumberlands a chance to show what they could do.

The plan of battle, according to Grant's memoirs, was to hit both ends of Bragg's line at once. Sherman was to attack Bragg's right flank and threaten his rear on Missionary Ridge. With luck, this attack would force Bragg to either weaken his line elsewhere or risk the loss of his supply base at Chickamauga Station. Meanwhile, Joe Hooker with his two corps from the Army of the Potomac would do similar service on Bragg's left at Lookout Mountain. When Bragg's forces were fully engaged with these flanking attacks, Thomas and the Army of the Cumberland would thrust for the centre of the line and break through – but if Thomas failed, just to threaten the centre would be enough to let Hooker and Sherman through on the flanks.

This simple plan was complicated by the terrain. Sherman had to cross the Tennessee to get to the northern end of Missionary Ridge, which involved crossing two other streams, the North and South Chickamauga. Since secrecy was important, this move was made at night, after a small force had been floated down-river in scows and landed to secure crossing points and capture the Confederate pickets. This meant building a number of pontoon bridges. Moving Hooker's men up would also be difficult and dangerous; Hooker's current task, keeping the Cracker Line open, was absolutely vital and taking him from it was a risk. Even so, this risk had to be taken and Hooker would move his men towards Missionary Ridge, keeping his troops in dead ground while maintaining a visible force on the river to attract the Rebels' attention. Such was Grant's plan; all the generals had to do was make it work.

On November 21 Grant took all three commanders to the north side of the Tennessee and showed them what he wanted them to do. On that day, news arrived that the battle for Knoxville had commenced so Grant hoped to start his battle on the following day; then the rains came and the rivers rose, putting the pontoon bridges under water. The attack was put back until November 24 and both divisions were over the river by daylight on that day. Meanwhile, on the morning of November 23 the Army of the Cumberland had taken a position called Orchard Knob, just outside Chattanooga, the jumping-off position for their assault on Missionary Ridge. The attack had been successful and Grant records that 'If I could only have been assured that Burnside could hold out ten days longer (at Knoxville) I should have rested more easily. But we were doing all we could for him and the cause.' That night, Sherman's force had also moved and was in position to advance on Missionary Ridge. Accounts of the battle for Chattanooga stress how anyone on the heights had an almost panoramic view of the battlefield and how the actions along the Ridge could be seen by all the participants. This being so, the somewhat frustrated troops of the Army of the Cumberland had to wait, forward of Orchard Knob, while the soldiers of Sherman's and Hooker's divisions opened the battle on the following day by assaulting the extreme flanks of Bragg's position. Hooker outnumbered the Confederates on Lookout Mountain by a considerable amount and his troops took the left end of the Confederate line as far as the crest of the mountain within a couple of hours and with few casualties. That night the Rebels evacuated Lookout Mountain and Hooker was able to switch his attack to the eastern side of the ridge.

At the other end of Missionary Ridge, matters went awry. Sherman's men went in, expecting to swarm up the slope and take the crest before them, only to discover that the visual crest concealed another crest. The top of Missionary Ridge was not a single ridge at all, but a series of outcrops and shallow valleys. Before long Sherman's troops were fighting across a series of hills and ridges, all lined with cannon and Rebel marksmen. The Army of the Tennessee chipped away at this position all day and got nowhere, and when they tried again on the following day, they did no better. Sherman reported to Grant that somehow the Rebel positions confronting him were being reinforced. Nor was Hooker providing much assistance; he brought his men forward towards the ridge but somehow they got lost in the woods and his attempt to come in on the Rebel left failed completely.

Grant watched all this happen from his position at Thomas's headquarters on Orchard Knob, puffing cigars, whittling wood, listening to reports brought in by the couriers, biding his time. Sherman remained convinced that the Confederates opposing him were being continually reinforced and was asking for more men but by mid- afternoon on November 25 it was clear that nothing much was being achieved on either flank – which brought Grant's eye round to the waiting and watchful troops of Sheridan's and Wood's divisions of the Army of the Cumberland, drawn up directly to his front. If these troops went forward and engaged the Rebel centre, Bragg could not continue to shore up the line facing Sherman. To climb the steep and well-defended slope of Missionary Ridge in front of the Orchard Knob was not a viable proposition, but a demonstration to the front of that slope might well do the trick.

Grant therefore ordered a limited advance. Thomas was to send his men forward and take the Confederate positions at the foot of the Ridge; if Sherman was right and the forces opposing him were indeed being reinforced, the reinforcements must be coming from somewhere – most likely the Confederate centre – and a threat there might call them back. Thomas duly sent his troops forward towards the foot of Missionary Ridge, where the Confederates had a strong position, with rifle pits, abatis, plenty of cannon and a good field of fire. This would be a close contest, but the wild card here that day was the mood of the Army of the Cumberland.

By this time, after days of baiting and name-calling from the soldiers in the other Armies, the men of the Army of the Cumberland felt they had something to prove – namely that they needed no advice from Western roughnecks or white-collared Potomac panty-waists when it came to fighting Rebels. The soldiers of the Cumberland had done their share of fighting in this war, and if matters had not gone too well for them lately, what of it? Simmering with rage, they shook out their battle flags and went into the attack with considerable vigour, clearing the Confederate positions at the foot of the Ridge in short order, the Rebels abandoning their lines and fleeing back up the Ridge. Very soon, says

Grant, 'loud cheering was heard as Wood and Sheridan were driving the enemy's advance towards Missionary Ridge'. There, at the base of the Ridge, according to Grant's clear instructions, the Cumberlands were to stop and await further orders.

But this was too much for them. There they were in the Confederate trenches and above them lay the crest of Missionary Ridge. The enemy were fleeing up that slope, and where they could go, the Cumberlands could follow. These were experienced Union soldiers and they recognised that, if they acted quickly, they could break the Rebel front. So the Cumberlands paused only briefly, to check their muskets. Then they clambered out of the Rebel trenches and advanced uphill to take the Ridge. This was, and remains, one of the most remarkable infantry actions in the history of warfare — an entire Army, attacking without orders, the men shouting 'Chickamauga! Chickamauga!' as they advanced to take their revenge for that recent defeat and show the other soldiers of the Union what good infantry could do.

'Without awaiting further orders or stopping to reform,' wrote Grant, 'our troops went to the second line of works, over that and then on to the crest, thus effectively carrying out my orders of the 18th for this battle and the 24th for this charge.' No one seems to have actually ordered this advance. It was started here and there by the junior officers – and the various regimental colonels made no attempt to check it – but mostly it came from the private soldiers, corporals and sergeants, and from the spirit of the Army. All the Cumberlands, from Phil Sheridan, who was there with his infantry division, down to the lowest private soldier in one of the battalions, appear to have been of one mind – to take Missionary Ridge. Up the slope surged the regiments, battle flags tilted forward, bayonets fixed, the men clawing their way up the slope on their hands and knees, scrambling and crawling over the rocks, ignoring the Confederate fire poured down upon them. The Army of the Cumberland were on their way to the top of the Ridge, and nothing was going to stop them but Death itself.

'The pursuit continued,' wrote Grant, 'until the crest was reached, and soon our men were seen climbing over the Confederate barriers at different points in front of both Sheridan's and Wood's divisions. The retreat of the enemy along most of his line was precipitate and the panic so great that Bragg and his officers lost all control over their men. Many were captured and thousands threw away their arms in flight.'

The Cumberlands' advance had nonetheless stunned Grant, Thomas and their staffs, all of whom were watching from Orchard Knob. Once he grasped what was happening, Grant turned furiously on Thomas, demanding to know who had ordered this second attack. 'Not me,' said Thomas. Grant then asked General Granger, one of the Cumberland corps commanders, if he had ordered it. Granger also denied responsibility, though he added that, once the Cumberlanders got going, they were hard to stop. Certainly, the Confederates could not stop them that day. Their advance up Missionary Ridge was a scrambling assault and units seem to have reached the crest of the ridge in different places at about the same time, urged over the crest by other units surging up behind. Once on top, they spread out to the flanks, winkling the Rebels out of their rifle pits, driving them back down the reverse slope. Within minutes, the Cumberlands had taken the crest of Missionary Ridge along almost two miles of front and, with his front broken, Bragg had no option but to order a retreat.

That night, Grant telegraphed Halleck that Bragg had been defeated at Chattanooga and that he would move at once to relieve Burnside at Knoxville. These moves had already begun, for even before the battle Grant had laid plans to follow this assault – which he assumed would be victorious – with an immediate move on Knoxville. Therefore, hardly had the cannon smoke cleared away from Missionary Ridge than Thomas had a steamer moving up the Tennessee loaded with rations and ammunitions to support Granger's Corps, which was marching for Knoxville along the bank. This steamer was to stay in close touch with Granger's IV Corps, which Grant had reinforced until its strength amounted to some 20,000 men.

Grant had kept this force on standby until he was sure Bragg was really in retreat, but on November 27 Granger was ordered to march at all speed for Knoxville. This Granger declined to do; he considered that his force was not sufficient to take on Longstreet's Corps, which was roughly the same size. Grant therefore ordered Sherman to march on Knoxville for, with Burnside's troops down to five days' supply of food, relief could not be delayed. Burnside was informed that Sherman was on the way and was determined to hold out until he arrived, but further resistance proved unnecessary. On hearing that Sherman was coming down on him, Longstreet lifted the siege of Knoxville and withdrew to the east at the end of November, closely pursued by Burnside.

These successes at Chattanooga and Knoxville caused elation in Washington, and President Lincoln wrote a warm letter of congratulation to his victorious general: 'Understanding that your lodgement in Knoxville and at Chattanooga is now secure, I wish to tender you and all under your command, my more than thanks, my profoundest gratitude, for the skill, courage and perseverance with which you and they, over so great difficulties, have effected that important object. God Bless you All.'

Lincoln's praise and gratitude were well-merited. Grant had around 60,000 men and Bragg about half that number but the Confederate position was said to be impregnable and Grant proved this wrong. He had fought a superb campaign, strategically and tactically, at Chattanooga, handling a diverse force in difficult terrain and always keeping his mind on the immediate problem – beating the Rebels at Chattanooga

– without being overly distracted by outside considerations such as the growing problem at Knoxville. On arriving at Chattanooga he had quickly taken a grip, sorted out priorities, secured the supply line, brought up reinforcements, developed an inevitably complicated plan to deal with the strong enemy positions and controlled his forces carefully until those positions had been overcome. Moreover, he had done this without great loss. Grant's total losses in the entire Chattanooga–Knoxville campaign – not including Chickamauga – came to 757 killed, 4,500 wounded and 330 missing. His forces had taken 6,142 prisoners, 40 guns and 7,000 stands of small arms – and driven the Rebels out of southern Tennessee, clearing the way for a Union advance into Georgia.

Admittedly, Grant had been helped by the ineptitude of Braxton Bragg. By sending Longstreet away to Knoxville with 20,000 crack troops, Bragg had fatally weakened his position around the besieged city, but at Chattanooga Grant revealed all the qualities that, in the year ahead, would mark him out as a great commander. It also helped that he was commanding some remarkably fine soldiers, and those of the Army of the Cumberland had no more trouble from the soldiers of the Army of the Tennessee after their day of glory on Missionary Ridge.

CHAPTER SEVEN

GRANT TAKES COMMAND
1864

It might be argued that the victory at Chattanooga was a soldier's battle, one gained by the valour of the ordinary fighting man rather than the acumen of the generals, but it takes a general – and a good one – to make a plan, organise a campaign, win a battle and follow it up. In the Union Army such men were in short supply, and their absence was noticeable. Halleck, for one, lamented the fact that he was without good commanders, although it is some indication of his chronic failure in judgement that he could make this remark about an Army that contained Grant, Sherman, Sheridan, Thomas, Meade, Sedgwick and Hancock. What was needed, however, was not more or better generals but one general with vision, to take command of the whole effort and create a viable strategy. This was really Halleck's job but he was never up to the task.

It was now the end of 1863, two and a half years into the war, and the Northern victories – be they outright, as at Vicksburg and Chattanooga, debatable, as at Antietam and Gettysburg, or barely concealed setbacks, as at Shiloh – were of no real use unless they were linked to the strategic prosecution of the war. That prosecution clearly depended on Lincoln's Administration finding a man who had the vision that all three previous commanders had lacked. If such a man existed, Lincoln must find him soon, for 1864 was bringing problems to the fore on the military and political front that would not brook delay and could give the Confederates the final victory in spite of the North's overwhelming military strength and economic power.

Just to begin with, 1864 was a re-enlistment year. Those tens of thousands of volunteers who had flocked into the Union Armies or been mustered into Federal service from the State militias in the spring and summer of 1861 had done so for a three-year term. Very soon those three years of service would be up, and unless those men volunteered again in their tens of thousands, President Lincoln might find himself without an Army. Of the 956 infantry regiments mustered into Federal service, no less than 455 would soon reach the end of their enlistment. Of 158 Union artillery batteries, men in eighty-one of them would soon be entitled to go home – and if they did so decide, there was no power in Washington to stop them. If the Northern Armies lost half their veterans, how could they hope to beat the men of the South?

Even as it was, the Union Army was changing and not for the better. The supply of volunteers had all but dried up and had been replaced by a form of draft. Only a form because it could easily be evaded, either for a while at least or for ever if the draftee could find someone willing to serve in his place or come up with $300 dollars to buy his release. As a result, apart from a quantity of draftees who were less than willing to fight but could be made into good soldiers, the Army began to fill up with 'bounty men', those who joined only for the enlistment bounty – which could go up to $1,000 in some states – and then deserted to enlist elsewhere on similar terms. Some bounty jumpers did this many times and made thousands of dollars before they were caught; none of them had any intention of serving in the front line. The veteran soldiers of 1861 detested the bounty men, who were, in the main, useless, and they knew that the survival of the Union largely depended on their own willingness to carry on the fight. If they could see that the war was being won, or at least sensibly conducted, enough of them might re-enlist.

Then there was another problem: 1864 was an election year. American Presidents then usually served just one term. To get re-elected, President Lincoln had to be renominated by his Republican Party – and this was by no means certain, for he was not universally popular in Washington and various other Republican contenders, including General Frémont and the Secretary of the Treasury, Senator Salmon Portland Chase, were eager to take on the job. Even if he was nominated, Lincoln had to be re-elected and there was plenty of opposition to him there, for his determination to win the war and save the Union were matched by that of those who believed that the war was too costly and that a negotiated settlement, even one accepting the existence of the Confederacy, might be a better solution.

Unless the war went considerably better than it had done so far, President Lincoln might find himself plain Mr Lincoln again, and the new incumbent at the White House, who would most assuredly be a Democrat, might soon be suing the Confederacy for peace. It was also clear that the peace party had a case. Three years of war and no apparent end to it, tens of thousands dead and hundreds of thousands wounded, and all for what? States' Rights or the Union? To coerce States that did not want the Union back into it? Freedom for the blacks – and if so, on what terms and would they know what to do with it? Was victory over the South worth it or, rather, would it work? Indeed, if the war could not be won but could only be continued at such a terrible cost, for no apparent gain, what other course was there but compromise with the South, surrender and partition?

One answer to this bleak election prospect was victory, for the North to muster all its strength and use it ruthlessly to win the war. Not necessarily a total victory in the coming months, followed by the total subjugation of the South – that was never on Lincoln's agenda – but at least some definite sign to the volunteer soldiers and the electorate that the Union cause was in competent military hands, that the Armies were being directed towards some achievable strategic end and that peace would come with the Union restored. That much might have seemed obvious, but three Generals in Chief in as many years – Winfield Scott, McClellan and now Halleck – had failed to deliver even a glimpse of a possibility that such a happy goal was attainable.

When the war started, the head of the Army was the Mexican War veteran, Winfield Scott – 'Old Fuss and Feathers' – an officer much loved by all ranks in the Regular Army, a good man in his day but long past his prime. Even so, he had made a start. Winfield Scott had ensured the Union Armies were sufficiently strong and well-equipped to avoid losing the war before it was fairly begun. Then Winfield Scott had retired and given place to 'Little Mac', General George C. McClellan, a man who had promised so much and given so little. Granted, McClellan had brought order and discipline to the army camps, reduced the death rates from sickness, introduced sound training programmes and restored the Army of the Potomac's confidence after various defeats. As a result, he was still remembered with affection by the Army of the Potomac and continued to command their loyalty. In some corner of their hearts, these Eastern soldiers would always be McClellan's Army. But McClellan had forgotten, if he had ever known, that the main purpose of a soldier – and especially of a commanding general – is to fight the nation's wars against the nation's enemies. McClellan had raised and trained and disciplined a mighty army, but he had no idea of how to use it. He always took counsel of his fears, believing, in spite of all the evidence, that the enemy was stronger, better prepared or better equipped than his own forces. The result of these fears was that he had allowed Lee to run rings round him, time and again, in battle and on campaign.

So McClellan had to go and then came 'Old Brains', fussy, nit-picking, bookish Henry Wagner Halleck, a commanding general who spent more time criticising his subordinates than helping them get on with the war. Halleck's reputation had been made by other men and by the end of 1863 his failings had been fully exposed. He was, at best, a competent staff officer, a good man with a pen, but totally useless commanding an army – or armies – where men must do their work with muskets, cannon and swords. As the war entered 1864, it was clear that Halleck, too, had to go. But who else was there? The Union had a quantity of competent generals – and a somewhat larger quantity of generals who were virtually useless – but one man stood head and shoulders above the rest, Major-General Ulysses S. Grant. In this extremity Grant was the only choice, the only soldier. This was not only the opinion of the President but the opinion of some of the other, hard-fighting Union generals – officers who were actively interested in getting on with this war and only needed some clear, uncluttered direction to deliver a victory. That direction could only come from one man, Grant.

Grant was an enigma. His most famous opponent, Robert E. Lee, once remarked that as the Union had tried half a dozen commanders for the Army of the Potomac, he was worried that they might one day chance on someone he could not understand. It is not likely that Lee failed to understand Grant, but when it came right down to it on the battlefield, Lee certainly could not handle him. Lee was not alone in this;

nobody could really figure Grant out, and yet the essence of the man as a professional soldier was clear. His talent was based on sound common sense, a clear realisation that a war and any battle in that war was only fought to be won.

The art of war, Grant once told a doctor on his staff, is simple really: 'Find out where the enemy is, get to him as soon as you can, with as much force as you can, strike him as hard as you can, and keep moving.' That clarity of vision, that ability to reduce the complexities to one clear philosophy, was the part of Grant that attracted the President. After Shiloh, when people came to him urging Grant's dismissal, the President's response was equally simple: 'I can't spare this man . . . he fights.'

It had taken time for Grant to rise so high in general esteem; he was totally lacking in charisma and those stories of his drinking never went away but in the end, by sheer ability, Grant came to the head of his profession. He arrived there at the hour of his country's greatest trial, for if Grant did not do well, the Union would lose more than a battle; they would lose Abraham Lincoln and, most probably, the war. So now Grant would be the General in Chief of the Union Armies. Vicksburg had suggested it, Chattanooga had endorsed it and Knoxville had confirmed it. His elevation seemed only to await some action by the President and the approval of the Senate.

There was a snag, though; Grant was a major-general. This was then the highest rank in the Union Army and the burden of command among its major-generals went by rank and date of appointment. If some other major-general entered Grant's bailiwick and that officer's commission pre-dated Grant's promotion, that officer would take command and Grant's competence would not come into it. Lincoln resolved the issue by promoting Grant to the rank of lieutenant general, the highest rank in the Army: only Washington and Scott – and Scott as a brevet lieutenant general – had ever risen so high. As a result, Grant's subsequent appointment to command all the Union Armies was unchallenged, if not entirely unquestioned, by the officer corps, although those old tales of his nights on the bottle did not entirely go away, especially in the Army of the Potomac.

Grant therefore came to Washington, checked in at the Willard Hotel and on the evening of March 9 1864 was invested with the Union command at a short ceremony in the White House. That done, Grant sat down to review the situation facing the Union at the opening of the campaigning season of 1864 and draw up plans for the work of his troops in the coming summer. One thing he was sure about: there would be no more one-off campaigns involving just one Army, a course which had enabled the South to move troops about to beat them; in the coming year, all the Northern Armies would be on the march, all the time.

The second thing Grant was sure about was that, General in Chief or not, he would not stay in Washington. Washington was not a town where Sam Grant felt comfortable. In the nation's capital he would be surrounded by politicians and placemen and those hard-faced men who were doing well out of the war, all of them attempting to get his ear. In Washington there would be committees and meetings and a round of social duties and receptions, all of which would eat up precious time. Washington was no place for a fighting general. No, Grant decided, Halleck would stay there as his chief of staff, to shuffle the paper, pass on the gossip, placate the Press and butter up the politicians; Halleck was good at all that.

Grant would establish his headquarters in the field, with the Army of the Potomac, first at Culpepper in Virginia, just south of Meade's headquarters at Brandy Station on the Alexandria to Orange Railroad. From here he would issue his commands – via Halleck – to all the other Union Armies, while taking a direct and personal interest in the affairs of

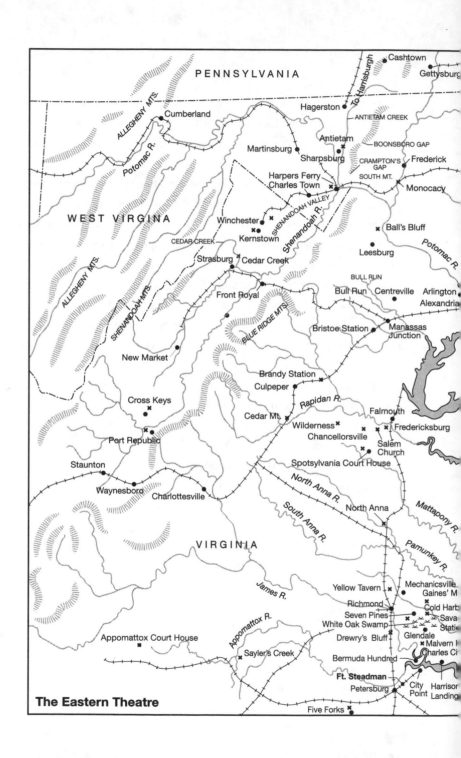

The Eastern Theatre

the main Union Army, the Army of the Potomac. Grant knew the one thing that had to be done was the one thing that had not yet been done. It was to do something about Robert E. Lee. In his report at the end of the war, Grant gave his views on the conduct of the war before he came to the overall command and his views on this point are crystal-clear:

> The Armies in the East and West acted independently and without concert, like a baulky team, no two ever pulling together, enabling the enemy to use the great advantage of his superior lines of communication for transporting troops from the East to West, reinforcing the army most vigorously pressed, and to furlough large numbers, during the seasons of inactivity on our part, to go to their homes and do the work of producing for the support of their armies. It was a question whether our numerical strength and resources were not more than balanced by these disadvantages and the enemy's superior position.
>
> I therefore determined, first, to use the greatest number of troops practicable against the armed force of the enemy; preventing him from using the same force at different seasons against first one and then another of our armies . . . Second, to hammer continuously against the armed force of the enemy and his resources until by mere attrition, if no other way, there should be nothing left to him but an equal submission with the loyal section of our common country to the Constitution and laws of the land.

When it came to applying this policy in the field, Grant saw the situation in early 1864 as follows. The Confederacy had two main Armies. The first and best was the Army of Northern Virginia, under Robert E. Lee. This was currently in winter quarters in Virginia, just below the

Rapidan river, positioned to guard the Confederate capital, Richmond. The second force was Joseph E. Johnston's Army of Tennessee, currently building up its strength in the north of Georgia. Johnston's headquarters were in the town of Dalton, close to Chattanooga, and his Army was charged with shielding the city of Atlanta. These two Confederate Armies were to be the prime targets for Grant's campaign in 1864. Only then would the Union forces worry about taking Richmond and Atlanta. If these two Armies, each mustering some 60,000 battle-hardened Rebel soldiers, could be destroyed and those two cities captured, the Confederacy would lose the war. To defeat these two Confederate Armies, Grant could deploy the main Union Armies under William Tecumseh Sherman and George Meade.

Sherman, who had taken over Grant's former command, was what would now be called an army group commander, for his forces – nominally the Grand Army of the West – consisted of three Armies: Grant's Army of the Tennessee, now under General James McPherson; the Army of the Cumberland under 'Pap' Thomas; and the smaller Army of the Ohio under John M. Schofield. The three Armies under Sherman totalled together some 100,000 men, more than enough to crush Joseph Johnston. In the East, George Meade, victor of Gettysburg, still commanded the Army of the Potomac, which, by the time Grant had reinforced it, would muster some 120,000 men.

There were other Union forces, armies, corps and divisions, which might also be profitably employed in the coming months. When it was all added up, Grant commanded 662,000 soldiers, the largest Army the United States had seen up to that time. This figure was, however, a gross amount; the net sum of men available in the rifle regiments was a good deal smaller. Trained and equipped troops, ready for battle, amounted to some 533,000 but then further numbers had to be deducted. There were some 40,000 in the North and West where no Rebels ever appeared. A number of regiments in the West were engaged in the continuing struggle with the Indian tribes and many more were engaged in protecting the lines of communication against the chronic scourge of Confederate raiding, a task which also reduced the available numbers in the field armies. 'Pap' Thomas's Army of the Cumberland, for example, had 102,000 soldiers on its ration strength in April 1864, but no more than 60,000 men were available to join Sherman when he set out to take Atlanta a month later.

Nevertheless, there were more than enough soldiers to overwhelm the Rebels if their commanders acted in concert. Grant was determined that this time at least the Union generals would all sing from the same song-sheet and direct their Armies to some common plan. This rule had to apply in particular to some of the smaller Union Armies. At the moment, General Nathaniel P. Banks, whose 40,000-strong Army should have formed part of Sherman's command, was still blundering about in Louisiana, trying to force its way along the Red River into Texas. This campaign had been ordered by the President, who was concerned at French activity in Mexico, and Grant could not call it off. General Ben Butler, one of the surviving political generals, was south of Richmond, achieving very little with his 35,000-strong Army of the James, but Grant intended to ginger him up by appointing General 'Baldy' Smith as one of his corps commanders. And there was Franz Sigel, another political general, important for securing the German vote but currently doing very little in the Shenandoah Valley where a competent general might – if properly directed and kept on a tight rein – have done a lot to reduce the South's fighting ability by destroying the food this valley supplied to Richmond and the surviving States of the Confederacy.

Then there were those various garrisons already mentioned, amounting to about a quarter of the entire Union Army, scattered brigades and divisions occupying ground or guarding railroads in those parts of the Confederacy recently taken by the Union Armies. These garrisons were currently on the defensive, simply holding ground taken by the field armies. Grant felt that they could perform this holding task equally well if they advanced against any Rebel forces in their vicinity and thereby stretched the Confederate forces even more. In short, all the Union forces must now go on campaign. Grant was missing no tricks, sparing no soldiers, letting no unit rest; this year all the Armies had to put their shoulders to the same wheel.

Grant's main strategic focus lay with the Army of the Potomac and Sherman's troops around Chattanooga, the two main arms of the vice that would crush the fighting strength of the Confederacy. Grant and Sherman knew each other well so there was no need for Grant to issue complicated or detailed instructions to this commander. Grant told Sherman to go for Joe Johnston and not to stop until Johnston had been driven from the field, his Army scattered and Atlanta in Union hands. As for the Army of the Potomac, that would go for Robert E. Lee and the Army of Northern Virginia and follow it wherever it went – and Grant would go with it.

This last decision might present certain problems. The Army of the Potomac saw itself as the senior of the Union Armies and Grant, for all his new eminence, was a Western general. The Army of the Potomac had fought hard and marched hard and survived plenty of defeats, and if it had not actually achieved a great many victories – or at least victories beyond all dispute or debate – it had done a great deal of fighting against the cream of the Rebel Armies. It was therefore less than sure about this new Western general who, it appeared, was not only the overall commander of the Union Armies but was also about to take a direct and personal interest in the actions of the Army, which was under General George Meade. Grant actually intended to sack Meade but, having met him and summed him up, Grant took a liking to him and left him in post.

There might still be a problem if the two men failed to agree but there was another one – dealing with Robert E. Lee. These Eastern soldiers, officers and men were not all that convinced that Grant was the right man for the job in hand. He might have taken Fort Donelson and Vicksburg, and he deserved credit for that, but there was a small cloud over the fight at Shiloh and rumour had it that Grant was supposed to drink. The plain fact, however, was this: Grant might have done well along the Ohio and the Mississippi, but it might be a very different matter when Grant came up against Robert E. Lee. Lee might be their enemy but, to the Union soldiers in Army of the Potomac, he was quite simply the best general in the war. Having fought him for two years, at Manassas, Antietam, Fredricksburg, Chancellorsville and most recently at Gettysburg, the officers and men of the Army of the Potomac were in a position to know all about the abilities of Robert E. Lee and the hard-fighting soldiers of the Army of Northern Virginia.

Grant was well aware of the reservations held about him by the soldiers of the Army of the Potomac. He was careful not to say that he had certain reservations about them. In Grant's view, when compared with the Western Armies, the Army of the Potomac had never quite managed to fight all-out, going headlong into battle in the way the Western Armies had done. In Grant's opinion, the Army of the Potomac was solid but without flair, ponderous but without gravitas; it needed some spark, a sense of superiority rather than resignation. Grant went with it because if – or rather, when – any hard decisions had to be made, he wanted to be on the spot to make them. It is much to the credit of Meade that he went along with this decision and accepted the inevitable outcome. From the spring of 1864, although Meade had the appointment, the effective commander of the Army of the Potomac was Ulysses S Grant.

Grant lost little time in getting to grips with the Army of the Potomac. With Lee as the target, he had it moved into camps along the Rapidan river, where the pickets were within earshot of the Confederate bugles. Grant also agreed with Meade's decision to reduce the number of infantry corps from five to three, largely because there were not five competent corps commanders in the Union Army. These three corps commanders would be Major-General W. S. Hancock, commanding the II Corps, Major-General G. K. Warren, commanding the V Corps, and Major-General John Sedgwick, commanding the VI Corps. In reserve for the moment but tasked later to guard communications was Major-General Ambrose Burnside's IX Corps.

With this reorganisation in place, there were marches to get the men fit and reviews so that the soldiers could see their new commander in chief and he could look at them. There were also more practical matters to which to attend. Grant was unimpressed by the cavalry of the Army of the Potomac. The cavalry regiments and brigades were split up among the corps and divisions and too many troopers were detached to serve as guards and escorts or on anti-guerrilla patrols. Grant formed the bulk of the cavalry into one corps and brought Phil Sheridan from the Army of the Cumberland to command it. He also combed out the back areas for fit soldiers on garrison duty and took a long step into the hearts and minds of the Potomac soldiers when he ordered that the gunners manning the heavy artillery in Washington should be rousted out of their warm billets, given a musket, taught some drill and sent to join the depleted infantry regiments on the Rapidan. Then there was plenty of drill and a great deal of firing practice; in previous battles too many soldiers failed to fire their muskets at the enemy or missed the enemy completely when they did fire. A lot of time on the ranges took care of that and so, as the first spring leaves appeared, the Army of the Potomac and Sherman's troops in the West prepared for their new campaign. In the process, the feeling grew among the rank and file that this general was someone who knew what he was doing and, maybe, this time, it would be all right.

Before the Armies could move, there was a bonus for Lincoln and Grant. By the end of April 1864, many of the men who had initially enlisted for three years came to the end of their time, yet nearly 200,000 of them, infantry, cavalry and artillery, signed up for another term. They had been urged to do this by their officers and the politicians of their home states, and offered inducements ranging from a cash bonus to a spot of leave and the right to call themselves 'veteran volunteers', but it is doubtful if such inducements made much difference. The money and the furlough were nice but the veterans stayed with their regiments and went back to the war mainly because they felt it was the right thing to do. These men had joined the Army to save the Union and they would not leave the Army until that job was done.

Grant now spelt out the campaign plan to his generals. The basic aim was simple for, as Clausewitz stated and Grant understood, in war only the simple succeeds. Every Army was to engage the enemy to its front. Lee was not to be given the chance to fight one enemy while the others hung back, and so to defeat the Union forces in detail. The campaign of 1864 was to be strategic and everyone must play a part. Sherman would march south through Georgia to take Atlanta. In the process, he would destroy Joseph E. Johnston's Army of Tennessee. Franz Sigel was to campaign in the Shenandoah Valley, destroying crops and cutting the railroad links with the South; without food the Confederacy would starve. Ben Butler would advance up the James, with Richmond as his focal point, while co-operating with the Army of the Potomac in the defence of Washington. Banks would come back

General Ulysses Simpson Grant, General in Chief of the Union Armies.
(*Hulton Archive*)

ABOVE Grant was always a superb horseman, skilled from boyhood in training and handling horses. Though noted for his horsemanship at West Point he was commissioned into an infantry regiment. (*Corbis*)

RIGHT The Battle of Shiloh was a very near-run thing for Major-General Grant. This stylised painting gives no indication of the chaos that actually prevailed. (*Hulton Archive*)

ABOVE LEFT General George B. McClellan – 'Little Mac' – was greatly loved by the soldiers of the Army of the Potomac, a force he raised and trained but had little idea of how to use in battle. (*Corbis*)

ABOVE RIGHT General Henry Wagner Halleck – 'Old Fuss 'n' Feathers' – was a fussy, nit-picking commander, with a reputation founded on the actions of other men. No friend to Grant when his superior officer, he proved adequate when serving on Grant's staff in Washington. (*Library of Congress*)

OPPOSITE ABOVE William Tecumseh Sherman was one of the best Civil War generals, and very loyal to Grant. 'Grant stood by me when I was crazy and I stood by him when he was drunk', he declared; his campaign in Georgia in 1864 was the decisive factor in securing Lincoln's election that year. (*Library of Congress*)

ABOVE The trenches and defences of Fort Sedgwick. This photograph shows how the sieges of the Civil War could have provided a foretaste of the fighting on the Western Front in France during the First World War, fifty years later. (*Library of Congress*)

LEFT This engraving of Federal gunboats running the Vicksburg batteries is a vivid picture of the risks taken to open up the Mississippi and start the campaign that led to the fall of Vicksburg in July 1863.

ABOVE LEFT President Abraham
Lincoln fought the war to save the
Union and was greatly relieved
when he found a general – U. S.
Grant – willing to fight the war
to a finish. (*Hulton Archive*)

ABOVE RIGHT General Joseph
E. Johnston was one of the best
Confederate generals, a stout
supporter of Robert E. Lee, but
unpopular with the Confederate
leadership in Richmond.
(*Library of Congress*)

LEFT Jefferson Davis. First
and only President of the
Confederate States of America.
(*Library of Congress*)

Robert E. Lee. Even during the war, Robert E. Lee was a hero to troops on both sides of the line, Union as well as Confederate. A superb general and a very fine man, he was only worn down by superior numbers – though doubts remain about his off-day at Gettysburg in 1863. (*Library of Congress*)

The surrender of the Army of Northern Virginia by Robert E. Lee to General U. S. Grant at Appomattox Court House, Virginia, April 9 1865. From a painting by Thomas Lovell (*Peter Newark's American Pictures*)

from Texas and follow Sherman while Grant would travel with the Army of the Potomac and deal with Robert E. Lee. These operations were to commence in early May and continue until all the objectives had been achieved.

Dealing with Lee presented Grant with a now familiar problem – how to get at him – but there was also one of supply. The two Armies confronted each other across the Rapidan but Grant had no intention of making a frontal assault on positions the Rebels had been developing all winter. This left him the choice of crossing the Rapidan above or below Lee's Army and attempting to flank him. Deciding which route was best was the most crucial decision Grant had to make before the Army went forward. If Grant moved by his right flank, swinging past Lee's left, he could follow the line of the Orange and Alexandria Railroad and quickly reach open country to the west. Alternatively, he could slip through the Wilderness, a region of secondary forest below the position now occupied by Lee's Army, and again reach open country, on the road to Spotsylvania. The attractions and difficulties of either route seemed equally balanced but the deciding factor was supply.

The first route meant relying on the Orange and Alexandria railroad, which Confederate guerrillas could easily cut. This would also remove the Army of the Potomac from all contact with Washington and Butler and oblige them to take every kind of stores with them, reducing the possibility of a rapid advance. Therefore Grant elected to go by the right of Lee's Army where he could be supplied from bases along the coast and keep in touch with Washington and Butler. He could also hope to get through the prime defensive country of the Wilderness and out into open country before the Rebels could intervene.

The Army of the Potomac, some 120,000 strong, moved out of its camps on May 4, marching down to the two Rapidan crossings with bands playing and colours displayed. From their observation points

across the river, the Confederate soldiers had been watching developments in the Union camps for some time and they watched the Yankee
soldiers coming on while preparing to move. Lee and his generals did
not intend to let the Union soldiers march unimpeded into Dixie. Lee's
plan was already formulated and when Grant moved, Lee moved also,
sending his men forward to confront the Union soldiers just across the
Rapidan in that hundred square miles of scrub, swamp and forest
Virginia people called the Wilderness.

CHAPTER EIGHT

THE WILDERNESS TO COLD HARBOR
May–June 1864

The campaign which Grant opened on May 4 1864 was different from all previous campaigns in this interminable civil war. Hitherto the Union general of an Eastern Army would take his force into the field and after the subsequent battle, win or lose, would march his depleted forces back into camp to rest and refit and try again another day. That option no longer existed in 1864 for the stakes were clearly higher this time. The campaign of 1864 would be the crucial campaign of the war. Unless the Northern Armies demonstrated that the war could be won, public and political pressure to end the war would rise this year, culminating when President Lincoln stood for re-election. Lincoln declared that he would not campaign for re-election since the issue of whether or not to continue with the war would be settled on the battlefield. Therefore, when his men marched across the Rapidan, Grant was beginning an election campaign as well as a military one; if the campaign foundered, Lincoln would lose that election and then the North would call off the struggle and settle with the South on whatever terms could be arranged.

Given hindsight, it is hard to see what settlement terms would have been either acceptable or workable. The position of the freed Negroes in Confederate States currently occupied by Union troops was one clear obstacle, for how could these people be returned to slavery? Were the Union to be dissolved and the former United States divided into two countries, what about the territories in the West that had yet to achieve statehood and join the Union? Would they be slave-holding states or free territory, Confederate or Union? Either way, they would be causes for dispute. What would be done about those slaves who, after partition, elected to flee to the North? Was it being suggested that the Fugitives Slave Act still applied and that runaway slaves must be captured by Northern sheriffs and shipped back to their masters?

These problems, and a hundred more, stood in the way of any nego-tiated settlement, one based either on allowing the Southern States back into the Union – on their own terms – or one based on partition. Not that this was really on the negotiating table; Northern politicians, Republican and Democrat, were in broad agreement that any settlement of the war must begin with the re-establishment of the Union – a demand to which the Confederate politicians in Richmond were com-pletely opposed. Clearly, the only way to settle this issue was with a Northern victory leading to re-establishment of the Union and full emancipation for the Negro. That task Lincoln had effectively delegated to Ulysses S. Grant.

In view of the high stakes involved, it is interesting to note in accounts from Lincoln's colleagues how relaxed and cheerful he was in the spring of 1864, a demeanour which was interesting but hardly surprising: the President's problems had been greatly reduced. At last, Lincoln had found a general he could work with, a man willing to prosecute the war and bring it to a victorious conclusion. One of Lincoln's secretaries, William O. Stoddard, later recalled Lincoln telling him, 'Stoddard, Grant is the first general I have ever had. He's a general . . . I don't know what his plans are and I don't want to know. I'm glad to find a man who can go ahead without me.' To find such a man must have been a great relief to the President at the start of this crucial year.

Therefore, although the soldiers did not know it, when the Army of the Potomac crossed the Rapidan in the spring of 1864, they were marching into a new kind of war. This was not just because they had a new commander – the Army of the Potomac had had plenty of commanders – but now they had a new kind of commander, a general who viewed war in a different kind of way to all previous commanders of the Army of the Potomac. Grant believed in total war, not just a series of disconnected, hopeful campaigns. Grant would wage war all the time with all his forces and bear down hard on anyone, soldier or civilian, who stood in his way. With this commander, there would be no turning back, no compromises, no retreats. This the Union soldiers had yet to discover but one of the Confederate generals, James Longstreet, who had served with Grant in the Old Army, knew it already. 'Grant will fight us every hour of every day until the end of the war,' he told his colleagues, and so it proved.

Grant did not, however, wish to fight the Rebel soldiers in the Wilderness, where the terrain would negate his advantage in numbers. The Wilderness, a broad stretch of tangled undergrowth, swamp and secondary timber about ten miles wide, spanned the country on the far side of the Rapidan. It began north of the right flank of the Army of Northern Virginia and reached south towards the village of Spotsylvania Court House. At the end of April, the fighting divisions of the Army of Northern Virginia lay to the west and behind the Wilderness, and Grant's first task was to get across the Wilderness as quickly as possible, before Lee could come forward. Then Grant could fight Lee in open country where the North's superior numbers could be used to best effect. This task would not be easy; there were few roads across the Wilderness and the two main roads, the Orange Turnpike and the Orange Plank Road, ran east to west; only one road, the Brock Road, ran in the direction Grant hoped to travel, south from the Rapidan towards Spotsylvania Court House and Richmond.

None of these roads was wide and to move an army of 116,000 men and 50,000 horses, infantry, cavalry, artillery and supply wagons through the Wilderness could not be accomplished quickly. Nor was that all. In the thickets of the Wilderness visibility in general was a few yards or at best, in the occasional clearing, perhaps a hundred yards. This was no place for a full-scale battle; artillery could not move here and where it could go there was no field of fire. The only way for any army to cross the Wilderness was in column of route down the roads, rapidly, by forced marches. The Union commanders, Grant and Meade, believed that the Army of Northern Virginia lay somewhere beyond the Wilderness, waiting in long-prepared entrenchments to resist the advance of the Union force, and Grant intended to outflank these positions by moving round them. It was a sound enough plan but it was not to work out like that.

Lee was an astute general and he had no intention whatsoever of letting Grant get his army through the Wilderness unchallenged to bring its full strength to bear in the more open country beyond. Grant's instructions to Meade – that the object of his advance was the Army of Northern Virginia and 'wherever Lee goes, there will you go also' – make Grant's strategy abundantly clear, but this strategy cut both ways. When Grant moved, Lee moved to meet him – and the two Armies met in the Wilderness.

The Union advance began on May 3. On May 4, the leading Union troops were across the Rapidan, moving well but at no great speed; if

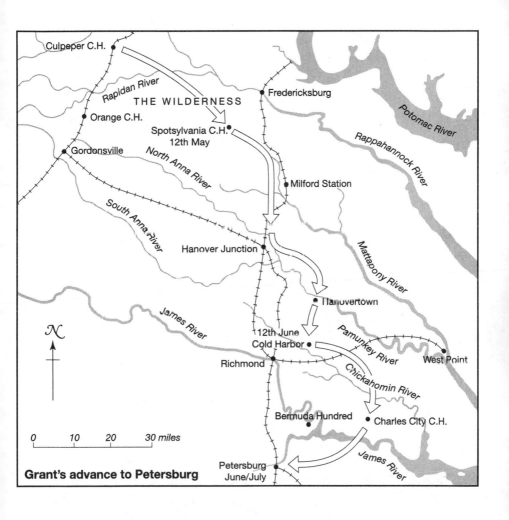

Culpeper C.H.

Rapidan River

THE WILDERNESS

Fredericksburg

Orange C.H.

Spotsylvania C.H.
12th May

Gordonsville

North Anna River

Milford Station

South Anna River

Hanover Junction

Mattapony River

James River

Hanovertown

N

12th June
Cold Harbor

Pamunkey River

West Point

Richmond

Chickahomin River

0   10   20   30 miles

Bermuda Hundred

Charles City C.H.

Grant's advance to Petersburg

Petersburg
June/July

James River

Potomac River

Rappahannock River

there was a sense of urgency, it fails to come through in the surviving accounts and only a few miles were made south of the Rapidan that day. The advance began again early on May 5, but then the divisions of Lee's indomitable Army came sweeping down the Orange Turnpike and the Orange Plank Road and hit the Union Army with the force of a runaway train.

The battle in the Wilderness began when the left wing of the Army of Northern Virginia hooked into the centre of the Army of the Potomac soon after dawn on May 5. Fighting began in the thickets astride the Orange Turnpike and by mid-morning the battle was in full flood. The Wilderness battle was confusing and must be seen as such; this was a scrambling affair, a kind of brawl, fought in thick undergrowth made even more impenetrable by clouds of musketry smoke, a hail of shot and before long, forest fires. Although most of the fighting took place along the axis of the two lateral roads, these could be covered by artillery and indeed were: they became vast bowling alleys down which cannon balls swept men away like ninepins. The infantry were therefore obliged to spill off the roads into the surrounding thickets where all order was quickly lost. This was the problem of the Wilderness battle. It lay not in finding and engaging the enemy, for he was everywhere and more than willing to fight, but in keeping a grip on one's own forces and fighting the battle with some degree of control – in finding gaps and feeding in troops to prise open the enemy position and get forward.

The first intimations that Lee's Army was in the Wilderness at all came at 0730hrs on May 5 when Confederate columns appeared from the west on the Orange Turnpike and were challenged by a skirmish line put out by Griffin's division of the V Corps. Hearing this, Meade ordered Griffin to attack with his whole division and drive the enemy back. Griffin tried but somehow nothing much happened until early in the afternoon when Griffin's division finally went forward and struck the advancing brigades of Richard S. Ewell's Confederate Corps. From that moment the battle of the Wilderness was on and the firing hardly stopped for the next two days.

The Wilderness was an infantry battle; one estimate has it that in the next few days some eighteen million rounds of small arms ammunition were expended in this violent engagement. In the woods and thickets, the sound of musketry rose to a crescendo that went on and on throughout the daylight hours, drowning the Union cheers and Rebel yells, yet failing to drown the cries of the wounded. Everywhere, confusion reigned. At one time it seemed as if Lee's Army would be cut in half; at another it was the Union Army that appeared to be in deep trouble, with at least one division totally lost and blundering about in the woods. Hancock's II Corps, which had swung wide from Chancellorsville to get into the battle, had to fight its way through a Confederate battle line to get into position. Warren was unable to get his V Corps forward to support Griffin, divisions sent forward got lost in the undergrowth, bumped into the enemy, formed a battle line and opened fire. This happened on both sides and by mid-afternoon on May 5, the battle was spreading like the brush fires it had started and was totally out of control.

So it went on all day and, as it went on, it got worse. Flaming wads from muskets set the dry leaves afire and little tongues of fire began to creep and thread their way across the Wilderness, setting the taller grass and bushes alight, creeping inexorably towards the many wounded men unable to move. By nightfall, the Wilderness was a mass of smoke and flame in which wounded men screamed for assistance as the flames came up and covered them. There was no pity here. Parties going out to help the wounded were ruthlessly shot down and at least 200 Union soldiers were burned to death as fires raged between the lines. The night itself brought little rest; the firing died down and men still tried to find and bring in the wounded, but the main task of the line and staff officers during the hours of darkness was to attempt to restore some order to this fight, to get the regiments into some sort of line, to find out what was happening now. This was in accordance with Grant's own, well-tested belief, that in any engagement there would be a pause and final victory would go to the side first able to renew the engagement.

At dawn on May 6 the main strength of the Union position seemed to be on the left, where Hancock's Corps was more or less complete and had some idea where it was going. The Confederates, faced with an easier defensive task, had other troubles to deal with, mainly that Longstreet's Corps was not yet up, Pickett's division had failed to arrive and A. P. Hill's Corps was short of men, ammunition and water. Therefore, when Hancock moved forward, Hill was obliged to fall back. He went as far as a clearing called Tapp's Farm on the right flank of the Rebel line, the place selected by Lee for his advance headquarters, just ahead of the Confederate supply train. Here was a Union opportunity: if the Tapp's Farm position could be taken, Lee would be without his supplies and obliged to fall back. Hancock therefore flung out his battle line and sent his men forward – straight into Longstreet's Corps, coming up at the run.

The Confederate artillery, massed here because there was no other place for it, was able to rake the Union line. This artillery fire, plus the wild charge of Longstreet's men, led by the Texas Brigade with Lee riding alongside, waving his hat to urge them on, stopped the Union advance in its tracks. Longstreet still had a grip on his Corps and he swung another brigade round into Hancock's flank. Struck in the front and flank, pounded by artillery, deafened by the Rebel yells, raked by a storm of musketry, Hancock's Corps stopped, hesitated, and fell apart. But as Longstreet's men pounded through the undergrowth after Hancock's fleeing troops, their own order was quickly lost. Hancock was then able to form a new front along the Brock Road that ran north to south across Longstreet's advance. Digging hasty trenches, throwing up breastworks of logs, the Union troops managed to form a line and when Longstreet's men came up, they were able to beat them off. The Union soldiers even managed to shoot Longstreet, who was taken to the rear badly wounded. Apart from a major assault on Hancock's position in mid-afternoon, this attack was the only move made by either side that day; Hancock's position held and the opposing forces settled down to the process of the day before, close-range musketry in the undergrowth – and again the fires started, spread and cooked those wounded men who could not crawl away.

The groping for position continued, each side feeling out the limits of the other's line. By late afternoon Lee had established that the right flank of the Union Army north of the Orange Turnpike, a position occupied by Sedgwick's Corps, was 'in the air' and open to attack. Lee duly found the end of that flank and at dusk, just as the firing was starting to peter out, he sent in Ewell's Corps. This struck Sedgwick's Corps on the flank and drove it in but fortunately Sedgwick was not prone to panic; like Hancock, he fell back, found a new position, rallied his troops, brought up his reserves and stabilised his front. By midnight the battlefield was almost silent, except for the unending crackle of the fire and the shrieks and moans of wounded men, thousands of them by now, lying untended in the woods.

There was no end to this, for the Wilderness battle was not going anywhere. There was no real order, no tactic for victory, just a series of reactions to events. Grant did little: his intention was to fight Lee and he was as willing to fight him here as anywhere else; the fact that his campaign had been halted on the second day did not greatly concern him. After two days of combat, the two Armies sprawled in a fire-stalked or burnt-out woodland, their divisions and brigades urgently in need of some order and direction – and that had to come from the top. Grant remained calm, smoking cigars and whittling wood, listening to reports, studying the maps, calculating what to do next. The only sign of anxiety came when an incautious staff officer from the Army of the Potomac remarked that Lee was sure to come in again with his whole force next day and get between the Union troops and any possible retreat to the Rapidan. Grant had heard just about enough of the Potomac soldiers' praise for Bobby Lee and retorted that he was 'heartily tired of hearing what Lee is going to do . . . it was time to think about what the Union troops were going to do and, having thought, get on and do it'.

Both Armies were fought out by the dawn of May 7. There was no major move that day, just a quantity of picket-line firing and a tacit truce to bring in the wounded. What was going to happen next depended on the commanders. By any previous standard, the Army of the Potomac had been beaten; casualties amounted to some 16,000 men and not a scrap of ground had been gained. The Union soldiers expected that, as so often before, their commanding general would admit defeat, give Bobby Lee the best of it and pull back across the Rapidan. But Grant had other ideas. Just after dawn on May 7, he wrote out his orders to Meade for transmission to the Army. These orders began, 'Make all preparations during the day for a night march to take position at Spotsylvania Court House.'

This intention was kept from the troops. That Grant would admit defeat and retreat was the general belief when orders to move were sent to the regiments on the night of May 7/8. The men were to move back, form up in column on the Brock Road and prepare to move out. Wearily, the men came back, grumbling that nothing much had changed, that Bobby Lee had outfought yet another Union general. They formed column, shouldered their muskets and prepared to march – and then Grant and his staff came jingling out of the night. The soldiers stepped back to let the horsemen past and then realised, suddenly, that Grant was riding *south*.

It took some little time for the Union soldiers to realise what was happening. Most of them had no idea which way they were facing when the march began but some did and the story quickly spread along the columns from regiment to regiment; Grant and the Army were indeed marching south. Spirits revived. Here and there regiments even began to cheer. Things were going to be different now. This was no defeat, simply because Grant would not accept defeat. The root of his strategy was pure attrition. The Wilderness casualties had been terrible but the North could afford such losses, if by affording them it hastened the end of the war, whereas the South could not. And it was just as well that the North could afford such losses, for they were about to mount.

Spotsylvania Court House, a major road junction, lies ten miles south-east of the Wilderness. If Grant could get to Spotsylvania before Lee, Lee would be in trouble, cut off from Richmond and forced to fight in the open. It took Lee a little time to realise what Grant had done, for Lee had lost almost as many men as Grant, was equally confused and equally encumbered with wounded. But when he realised that Grant had moved south, he saw at once that this move could be deadly. At Spotsylvania the Union Army could force Lee onto the offensive – an offensive which, given the disparity in numbers, he could not hope to win. Equally disastrous would be for Grant to drive Lee back inside the defences of Richmond, for that would bring on a siege and rob Lee of any chance to manoeuvre.

Lee had already remarked that if Grant reached the James river, the Army of Northern Virginia would be obliged to withstand a siege – 'and after that it will be a mere question of time'. Lee was a fine tactician with an eye for ground; to exploit these talents he needed to pick his own ground for a fight and exploit the skill and valour of his incomparable infantry. If attacking the enemy was expensive, losing the ability to move would be fatal. Lee had, however, the faults of his virtues. He was a combative commander, preferring attack to defence, however costly or ill-advised; at Gettysburg his offensive spirit had led to the loss of Pickett's division and the whole battle on the third day – and Lee was about to make the same mistake again. Perhaps he lacked direction from the top, for the strategic situation was political as much as military. The most important task for the Confederate armies in 1864 was to deny victory to the Union. If they could do that, scoring successes without great loss to themselves, sickening the Northern electorate with further pointless slaughter, Lincoln would fall in November and peace on acceptable terms was more than possible. Joseph Johnston, facing Sherman's Army of the Tennessee in Georgia, had already grasped this point; Lee in Virginia had not.

Lee and the Army of Northern Virginia were more than just two military components, army and commander; the whole was much greater than the sum of the parts. Together they had been able to out-think, out-march, out-manoeuvre and, so far, out-fight any Army that came against them, but to do this Lee and his Army had to be able to move. If Grant could crowd them into a corner or force a siege, as Lee said, it could only be a matter of time. This being so, Lee took the next worst option, to fight Grant in the open. He pulled his Army out of the Wilderness and just beat Grant to the crossroads at Spotsylvania Court House.

It was a near-run thing. The battle at Spotsylvania began with a skirmish between advance guards and flared up into another all-out, no-holds-barred battle that went on for ten full days, much longer and in some ways much worse than the Wilderness fight had been. At Spotsylvania there was room to deploy cannon and manoeuvre large bodies of troops. Having been denied the vital crossroads, Grant's aim was to hook round the right flank of the Confederate Army and get the Union Army between Lee and Richmond. Lee was equally determined to stop him, so the Armies surged in and swung about each other, circling always to the right, from Spotsylvania to North Anna to Cold Harbor. In fact, they completed almost half a circle; units facing south-east when the battle began were facing north-west when it ended. The crux came on May 12, in the fight for a set of Confederate trenches covering the main road junction, a position known as the 'Bloody Angle'.

Everything was flung into the fray at the Bloody Angle. Men fought hand-to-hand with musket and bayonet, sword and pistol. Charge followed counter-charge; the dead and wounded piled up four-deep before the Confederate barricades and in the Confederate trenches; even mature trees were cut down by musket fire. Union cannon were trundled up to the Rebel line, loaded with canister and fired at point-blank range into the Confederate trenches before the gun crews were shot down. It was sheer madness.

The fight for this one small position lasted a whole day and when it was over all the Union had to show for it was half a square mile of torn ground and the bodies of 5,000 dead or wounded men, including General John Sedgwick, shot down at long range by a Rebel sharpshooter. On the other hand, outside the main battle, Sheridan's cavalry at Yellow Tavern, striking towards Richmond, had finally killed the Confederate cavalry general Jeb Stuart. So the killing went on, but none of it seemed to make any difference. And yet there was a difference. The Army of Northern Virginia, that bright and flexible instrument, the sword of the Confederacy, was not fighting as it was accustomed to fight, for the terms of this battle were being dictated by Ulysses S. Grant. To use a boxing maxim, Grant was all over Lee, pressing him hard, using his weight to keep him pinned. Lee was unable to break off the fight, to push his opponent back and gain space to move. This was the kind of all-out fight in which, at the end of the day, 'the good big 'un will always beat the good little 'un'. Lee was still able to fight well. He was not losing this fight but after two weeks of constant fighting he was not winning it either – and there was the difference.

No battle in this war had lasted so long. The Armies fought on, day after day, out of the Wilderness and south to Spotsylvania and then south again across a series of small rivers that never quite offered Lee enough of a line to hold on to, not on the North Anna, or the Pamulkey or, at the end of May, the Chickahominy. Losses were terrible: in the first thirty days of the 1864 campaign in Virginia, Grant lost over 50,000 men, almost twice as many as Lee, but Grant could afford to, for replacements were coming down steadily from Washington. Marching and fighting, always trying to get round Lee's right flank, Grant pushed the Confederates back until the Armies moved out into the flat, half-drained swamps around the Chickahominy, close enough to hear the church bells from Richmond on Sunday. And so, in early June, they arrived before the little town of Cold Harbor.

At Cold Harbor Grant judged it right, in terms of time and place and his available force, to bring the Confederates to battle and crush Lee once and for all. Lee's Army was much reduced and very tired, and however much Lee might wish to avoid a fight to the finish, he had his back to the Chickahominy, beyond which lay Richmond. Lee had to stand here and this, thought Grant, was a good place to fight him and win. But Grant did not win. On June 1 and again on June 3, the blue lines went forward against the Confederate defences, and both assaults were disasters. The two-day pause between the attacks was the real problem. Lee was a great believer in the spade and the Army of Northern Virginia had been given a full day to dig in; in that time they had built breastworks and cleared a wide field of fire at Cold Harbor, the perfect killing ground if the attack was renewed.

The great tactical lesson of the Civil War – that resolute men in trenches, when armed with a rifled musket capable of killing men at ranges of up to half a mile, could not be dislodged by any means currently available – was learned yet again before Cold Harbor. In his memoirs, Grant recalls the second assault at Cold Harbor as his worst mistake in the war. The casualty figures support that judgement: Union losses exceeded 7,000 men that day and Confederate losses were probably below 1,500. And yet, on balance, Grant was well satisfied with the campaign so far. The battle had been fought his way and his strategic intention, to push Lee south and form a junction with Ben Butler and the Army of the James, was still possible. If it had been costly to the Union, the Confederate side, although suffering smaller losses, had fewer men to lose. 'The result of the three-day fight in the Old Wilderness was decidedly in our favor,' he wrote in his first despatch to Washington on May 8. This opinion had not changed by the time of his next despatch on May 11:

> We have now ended the sixth day of very heavy fighting. The result to this time is much in our favor. But our losses have been heavy, as well as those of the enemy. We have lost to this time eleven general officers, killed, wounded and missing, and probably twenty thousand men. I think the loss of the enemy must be greater, we having taken over four thousand prisoners . . . I am now sending back to Belle Plain all my wagons for a fresh supply of provisions and ammunition and propose to fight it out along this line if it takes all summer . . .

After Cold Harbor, not everyone agreed with Grant's confident assessment. The losses were far higher than he claimed – Grant had lost an average of around 2,000 men, killed or wounded, every day of this campaign, a Great War rate of loss, and this quantity could not be concealed. The Peace Democrats were already calling him 'Butcher Grant' and pointing out that his victories, if victories they were, were of the Pyrrhic kind; something more than this would be needed to win the election for Lincoln. As it was, the slogging, costly advance from the Wilderness came to a stop for a while at Cold Harbor, where the Union soldiers dug in and a siege began. They had fought Lee's Army for a full month, from May 4 to June 3, and hurt it grievously, though at great cost to themselves; now a pause was needed before they fought him again.

CHAPTER NINE

ATLANTA AND PETERSBURG
June–September 1864

Although he was closely engaged with Lee in Virginia and effectively commanding the Army of the Potomac, Grant never forgot that he was the General in Chief of all the Union Armies, responsible for the entire military effort of the Union side, as well as for liaison with the Navy – and for giving President Lincoln the victory he needed in order to maintain the war. The roar of cannon should not be allowed to conceal the fact that Lincoln's re-election was the crux of the Union problem in 1864 and his success at the polls depended on victory in the field. This would remain the case, a fact Lincoln put in a letter early in September of that year:

> This morning, as for some days past, it seems exceedingly probable that this administration will not be re-elected. Then it will be my duty to so co-operate with the President-elect as to save the Union between the election and the Inauguration; as he will have secured his election on such ground that he cannot possibly save it afterwards.

Such political considerations aside, Grant was responsible for directing the higher strategy of the war on every front, and with the Army of the Potomac stalled in the trenches at Cold Harbor and unable to offer any aid to the beleaguered President, his focus of attention shifted to the other main theatres of war, along the James and in the Shenandoah Valley, and especially to the actions of his most loyal and trusted subordinate, William Tecumseh Sherman, and his Army Group in the West.

A few days after Grant crossed the Rapidan, Sherman led his combined army – troops from the Army of the Cumberland under Thomas and the Army of the Tennessee under McPherson – out of their camps around Chattanooga and began to march them south and east in the general direction of Atlanta, the capital of Georgia, a hundred miles away. Sherman had a strong force of some 90,000 men, all veterans, and he would need every one of them for between Chattanooga and Atlanta stood Joe Johnston and his Army of the Tennessee with some 60,000 men. Most of these Confederate soldiers were dug in to await both events and Sherman's Army on a range of hills north of Dalton known as Rocky Face Ridge, a position which was crossed by the Chattanooga to Atlanta Railroad at a gap called Buzzard's Roost.

Sherman and his men duly came up to Rocky Face Ridge. Having viewed the Confederate position, Sherman sent in solid, reliable 'Pap' Thomas and around 60,000 men from the Army of the Cumberland, with orders to prise the Rebels loose. Thomas tried hard, but the Rebel position was too strong, he was beaten off with loss and Sherman called the battle off. Sherman was combative, but canny. He had no intention of wearing his Army down with frontal assaults at this stage in the campaign, certainly not if there was another way to do it. 'Sweat saves blood' is an old military maxim and Sherman therefore sent McPherson and his Army of the Tennessee on a fast, pounding march around the Ridge, a flanking march that brought them to the town of Resaca, ten miles

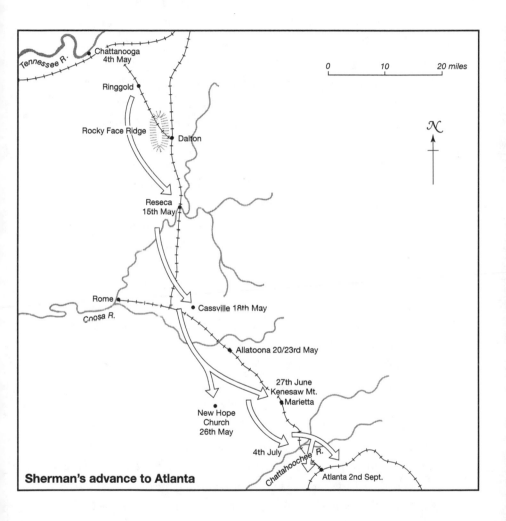

Sherman's advance to Atlanta

south of Dalton and well behind Johnston's lines. Sherman was delighted with this strategy. He felt that he had put Johnston in the bag, but the Confederates were equally light on their feet. Within a day, Johnston's Army had pulled back, staved off McPherson's force and got away to the south – and it all had to be done again. This event set the pattern for their midsummer dance across the South. Sherman remained firm in his resolve not to mount direct attacks but to lever the enemy line loose with flanking marches; Johnston was equally determined not to let Sherman box him in.

Sherman was right to avoid frontal attacks because these flanking marches were taking his troops in the direction they had to go – south towards Atlanta – and obliging Johnston to give up valuable ground. For his part, Johnston was well aware that the main Confederate objective at this time was – or should have been – to deny the Union side victory and keep the Confederate forces in being. If that meant giving up ground, so be it; avoiding defeat before the November election in the North was the sensible policy. Yet this policy was not understood in Richmond. The Confederate President, Jefferson Davis, had little time for Joe Johnston, thinking him an over-cautious general, and Davis grew increasingly worried as Sherman's men marched deeper into Georgia and began to threaten Atlanta, the second city of the South.

The Army of the Tennessee could fight but it could also march and dig, and marching and digging were the qualities it needed now. The tactic Sherman evolved that summer required Thomas's Army of the Cumberland to form a front and keep the enemy pinned, while McPherson took the Army of the Tennessee round their flank and forced another withdrawal. It was not very showy and it meant a lot of extra miles and a lot of sweat, but it worked. Slowly, inexorably, the Union Armies drew closer to Atlanta while avoiding frontal assaults.

All this took time, and before the month of May was out, there was a certain amount of grumbling, in both Richmond and in Washington. From Washington, where all eyes were on the electoral clock, came complaints that while some ground was certainly being taken, not much was being done to settle accounts with Johnston's Army. Similarly, Johnston was getting complaints from Richmond that unless he could stand and make the Union Army fight him – and beat it when it did so – he would soon find himself retreating through the peach orchards of Atlanta – and if that city fell, the North would have their victory anyway. Nor were the Union soldiers all that happy. May was pleasant enough but most of June was spent enduring heavy rains that turned the Georgia roads into quagmires and held up the forward movement of supplies. There were a few stand-up fights and a tough, three-day affair at New Hope Church that cost both Armies a quantity of lives but by the end of June, Sherman felt that his Armies had done enough of these relentless marches and should now oblige the enemy with a frontal assault. This was something else Grant and Sherman had in common: a basic eagerness to fight. They could use their heads and conduct successful campaigns of manoeuvre but it went against the grain; sooner or later their patience snapped and they gave in to the urge for battle. Unfortnately, the place Sherman chose to launch his offensive was no better than Cold Harbor. At Kenesaw Mountain the ground favoured the defence and the Confederate defences were extremely strong.

The Confederates had dug themselves in on the top of the mountain, behind a glacis of tree trunks and a network of trenches, and when the Federal lines came over the crest on June 27, Rebel guns and musketry blew them away in large numbers. By the end of the day, the Union had lost 3,000 men and 'Pap' Thomas was right to tell Sherman that 'one or two more such assaults will use up this entire army'. Sherman attempted to shuffle off the blame for this defeat onto Thomas, telling Grant that the Army of the Cumberland was 'dreadfully slow. A fresh furrow in a plowed field will stop the whole column and all begin to entrench', but that excuse would not wash. The attack on Kenesaw Mountain was a mistake and even though the Union side had managed to kill the veteran Confederate general, Leonidas Polk, it was clear that there was no way through the defences of Kenesaw Mountain if the Rebels were determined to hang onto them. This being so, it was back to the old tactic; flanking marches and plenty of digging.

And yet, in a way, this whole campaign was a Union victory. Twelve days later, on July 9, Joe Johnston did indeed find his Army among the peach orchards of Atlanta and was forced to put his soldiers into trenches to defend the city. His room to manoeuvre was at an end, and so too, for a while, was his career; the arrival of the Union Armies at Atlanta was regarded in Richmond as a strategic defeat. Jefferson Davis was furious and on July 17, Joseph Johnston, one of the best generals in either Army and a man who saw the current strategic problem clearly, was relieved of his command and replaced by the General, John B. Hood.

Hood was a veteran of Gettysburg, where one of his arms had been crippled, and Chickamauga, where he had lost a leg, but these grievous wounds had done nothing to blunt his appetite for battle. He was no strategist and caution was not part of his nature. Hood was more warrior than general and his usual reaction on sight of the Union enemy was to fling out his battle lines and send the regiments forward, regardless of the situation, regardless of loss. He would fight Sherman all day, every day and twice on Sunday, and it was this part of his character that Sherman hoped to turn to Union advantage. If it had proved hard to provoke an all-out fight with Joe Johnston, it would prove no trouble at all to provoke John B. Hood.

On July 19, Sherman sent his men across the Chattahoochee river, pointing them directly towards Atlanta. He was now applying his usual tactic, sending Thomas and the Army of the Cumberland directly across

Peachtree Creek into the city while McPherson and the Army of the Tennessee set out on another of their flanking marches towards Decatur, aiming to cut the roads leading into the city and approach Atlanta from the east. This was all it took to get Hood moving. On July 20, when Thomas was getting his men across Peachtree Creek, just five miles from the centre of the city, Hood came down on him like a thunderbolt, with every man and musket in his command.

This was an encounter battle, between two Armies on a collision course, the kind of battle at which Thomas excelled; not for nothing was Thomas known as the Rock of Chickamauga and he was determined to hold his ground. Thomas was not about to panic; like Sherman, he knew Hood's character well and this violent attack was not unexpected. Although the attack came in when Thomas had only one corps across the creek, he was able to cover the crossing with his artillery, then feed more guns across to form an artillery line while his infantry deployed. Artillery fire broke up the first waves of the Rebel attack, and with that done, more Union troops were sent across the river. By nightfall, both sides had taken casualties but Hood's attack had been held.

Held but not defeated. If there was no advantage to be gained by striking at Thomas, now dug in behind a strong line of artillery, Hood would try his hand at McPherson, who had gone off to the east while Thomas was engaged at Peachtree Creek. McPherson was at Decatur, five miles east of Atlanta, coming in towards the city with less caution than he might have used, being convinced that Hood was fully occupied with Thomas. McPherson was a good general – he would not otherwise have lasted long under Grant and Sherman – but on July 22 Hood took him unawares and drove him back. If McPherson thought Hood was too closely engaged with Thomas to spare any attention to the approach of the Army of the Tennessee, the volume of musket and cannon fire to his front that day told him differently. McPherson therefore rode to the front to take charge of the action and was promptly shot from his horse by a party of Confederate skirmishers. Even so, the Union line held and the Confederate advance was stopped by General John A. Logan, who now took command. It took the Army of the Tennessee all day to blunt Hood's attack and then only at considerable cost, while the death of McPherson, a first-class general who could ill be spared, reduced even the grim Sherman to tears.

Having halted Thomas and Logan, Hood retreated into the defences of Atlanta while Sherman considered his options. So far, Hood had had the best of it. He had fought off two Union Armies in rapid succession and held Atlanta. It might have been possible for Thomas to push on into Atlanta on July 22 when Hood was busy with McPherson, but Sherman wasted no time in brooding over might-have-beens. He sent Logan and the Army of the Tennessee on another of their flanking marches and on July 28 they came in against Atlanta from the west, running into Hood again at Ezra Church, where the two Armies fought yet another brisk and costly engagement. That made three battles around Atlanta in rapid succession. Hood's Army was almost fought-out but the Rebels were still full of fight. 'How many of you are there left, Johnny?' enquired a Union soldier of a Rebel picket. 'Oh, about enough for another killing' was the reply. This was all too true.

To conserve numbers, Hood was obliged to quell his natural combativeness and send the remains of his Army into trenches and withstand a siege. Sherman was also willing to pause and while the men on both sides plied their spades again, he replaced Logan – who did not get on with his colleague, 'Pap' Thomas – with General Otis Howard. Howard had no particular flair but could handle a siege and Sherman trusted him to maintain the pressure on Hood. Atlanta was surrounded, heavy guns were brought up and set to pounding the defences, and the Union positions slowly shifted to cut all the roads leading into the city.

With starvation looming, the fall of Atlanta was only a matter of time.

Time, however, was the problem. Back in Washington, the President did not have it. It was now August, the election was drawing ever nearer and where was the evidence that this war could ever be brought to a successful conclusion on the battlefield? Three months of all-out fighting, terrible losses, Northern hospitals crammed with wounded, and what was the result? Stalemate, on both main fronts. Both Union Armies had now ground to a halt and by midsummer the smart money in Washington was on a defeat for Lincoln and the election of a Democratic candidate – General George B. McClellan, if he would stand – on a policy of accommodation with the Confederacy.

Nor were matters going well elsewhere. The other Union commanders had moved simultaneously but none had advanced successfully. Banks had made a total mess of the campaign on the Red River in Louisiana, in spite of the loan of 10,000 soldiers from Sherman's Army. Everything went wrong, the Confederates thrashed Banks at the Sabine Cross Roads and Banks was replaced by Major-General Edward R. S. Canby. In Virginia, Ben Butler had duly put his 30,000-strong forces ashore on the Bermuda Hundred on the James river, south of Richmond on May 5, acquiring a number of options. He could move directly on Richmond, he could seize Petersburg, the railroad centre that supplied the capital, or he could put his forces astride the road and rail links between Richmond and Petersburg and thereby ensure the eventual fall of both. But Ben Butler did none of these things. He wasted time and dispersed his forces, making small, ineffective jabs at all three objectives until the Rebel commander on the James, General P. G. T. Beauregard, had managed to assemble a sufficient force – smaller than Butler's, but more than adequate to hold him off.

Grant was well aware of Butler's basic incompetence but had hoped that the two subordinate generals in Butler's force, Generals Smith and

Gilmore, would compensate for their commander's deficiencies. This did not happen. On May 16, Butler finally moved on Richmond, only to get a bloody nose from Beauregard's troops, now snugly dug in behind earthworks. Beauregard then came out and struck Butler hard, driving him back with the loss of 4,000 men. Butler withdrew inside the defence lines of the Bermuda Hundred, a peninsula on the James river – and Beauregard promptly came up and dug a new Confederate defence line across the neck of the peninsula. Grant remarked that Butler's Army was now as much out of the war 'as if it had been in a strongly corked bottle'. Having taken care of the threat from Butler, Beauregard was then able to send 7,000 men north to help Lee, a most useful reinforcement.

These were not the only reinforcements reaching Lee. Another 2,500 hardened veterans arrived from the Shenandoah Valley, where the Confederate general John Breckenridge had defeated Sigel at Newmarket on May 15 and driven him back up the valley, in headlong retreat for more than twenty-five miles. Two elements in Grant's campaign strategy for 1864 had fallen apart in the first month and by August, Grant and the Army of the Potomac, having left Cold Harbor, were held before Petersburg. Now it all depended on Sherman.

Granted, there had been a victory of a sort in Mobile Bay, where Admiral Farragut was able to score a small but useful success in early August, sinking the remains of the Confederate Fleet. Farragut was aware that land forts had no effect on ironclad warships and he was able to ignore their fire and enter the Bay, thereby closing Mobile, the last Confederate sea port and a target on Grant's list since 1862. This provided a fillip for Republican morale in the North, but not enough to swing a sizeable amount of votes for the new 'Union Party' – which was actually the Republican Party but so called in the hope that a change of name and mention of the Union would attract Democratic votes.

Meanwhile, Grant had moved south from Cold Harbor. He had

stayed in trenches there for two weeks but his strategic aim had not changed. Grant was determined to destroy the Army of Northern Virginia. He also intended to link the Army of the Potomac with the Army of the James and then cut the Confederacy off from its capital, specifically by taking the rail junction at Petersburg – and that meant crossing to the south side of the James river and getting Butler out of the Bermuda Hundred. That in turn meant moving the Army of the Potomac away from its current position outside Cold Harbor – and this move would be eased if those parts of this strategic plan currently in disarray could be put in some sort of order.

Therefore, Sheridan was ordered to take the cavalry corps in a sweep around Richmond, destroying every piece of railroad equipment and railroad track he came across. Then General David Hunter was sent to the Shenandoah Valley with instructions to round up the remnants of Sigel's defeated force, meet up with General Crook in West Virginia, then join Sheridan and come south to join Grant. Unfortunately, this new scheme did not work out. On June 5, Hunter destroyed a Confederate force at Piedmont and killed its commander, General W. E. Jones. This defeat and the possibility that the Union would succeed in overrunning the Shenandoah – the breadbasket of the Confederacy – thoroughly alarmed Richmond and on June 7 reinforcements were sent to the Valley, with orders to stop Hunter in his tracks, which they were able to do at Charlottesville. On the same day, Sheridan set out on his raid, and both these moves provided a useful distraction while Meade pulled his Army out of the siege lines at Cold Harbor and struck south to the James.

This move began on June 12, led by the only cavalry division Sheridan had left with the Army of the Potomac which cleared away the Confederate pickets and opened the road for Warren's Corps. When Lee discovered that the Union Army were marching towards Richmond, south of the Chickahominy, he assumed that this was yet another of

Grant's flanking movements, one aiming directly at the Confederate capital. This had to be an assumption, for Lee's scouts were unable to penetrate the Union cavalry screen and find out exactly what Grant and Meade were doing. And until Lee knew exactly where Grant was heading – to Richmond, north of the James, or Petersburg, south of it – he could not bring his Army into position to oppose him.

Finding the answer took some days. The Army of the Potomac was happy to be out of the Cold Harbor lines and marched fast, breaking contact with Lee's forces. The aim was to cross the James by a hastily constructed causeway and on June 15 Hancock's Corps led the Army of the Potomac over the river, and while Meade's Army was crossing the James, Grant went by steamer to the Bermuda Hundred to confer with Banks. Butler had been making a few moves, sending General Gilmore and some 5,000 men out on June 9, to see if the defences of Petersburg could be stormed. Gilmore concluded that they could not and returned without attacking – and Butler promptly sacked him. Butler's other subordinate general, 'Baldy' Smith, was available with his corps of some 16,000 men, and Grant told Butler to send Smith over the Appomattox river on June 16 and put in a solid attack against the Petersburg defences, while Hancock came up in support from the Army of the Potomac. This would raise the Union force attacking Petersburg to some 35,000 men against the possible 9,000 that, according to Union estimates, Beauregard currently had in his defences – and Lee was still at Cold Harbor, too far away to intervene.

The Union estimate of Rebel strength at Petersburg was wildly out. Beauregard only had some 2,500 men – and even without Hancock's men, Smith had nearly 17,000 soldiers, most of them seasoned veterans. Had matters been handled with even a modicum of competence, Petersburg should have fallen to the first assault, but competence was lacking. This was when Grant realised Smith's limitations, for this failure destroyed the reputation Smith had acquired at Chattanooga. It was the familiar problem: a certain hesitation, a total lack of grip, an unwilling-ness to probe the enemy position and get into it. Smith spent a great deal of time studying the ground – a wise enough move normally but not when speed was of the essence. Then it was discovered that the Army of the James's artillery commander had not been kept informed and so had sent all his horses off to water, thereby delaying the attack until the evening. Hancock, who had never fully recovered from the wound he had sustained at Gettysburg, also seemed to be suffering delays. What with one thing and another, the attack against the Petersburg defences did not go in until dusk – when it was a great and unexpected success.

Within an hour of advancing, Smith's men had taken a mile and a half of trenches, several pieces of artillery and a quantity of prisoners. The Union soldiers were already well inside the Confederate lines and only had to push on to enter Petersburg and stand on the railway tracks; as General Beauregard said later, 'Petersburg was at the mercy of the Federal commander, who had all but captured it.' This fact totally escaped Smith's notice; darkness came on, Smith became cautious and overnight Beauregard was reinforced by Lee; by dawn, the defenders of Petersburg could muster around 7,000 men, a force that grew even stronger when Beauregard elected to abandon the lines outside the Bermuda Hundred and concentrate his forces for the defence of Petersburg. They had time to get there, for Smith did not move until 1800hrs on July 16, when Meade ordered Hancock to assault the town.

Hancock's Corps struck hard and gained a little ground but they were then held. Slowly, over June 17, the Union advantage began to slip away as Lee, realising what Grant intended, arrived to take up the chal-lenge. The problem was the one Grant had always suspected: there was a lack of initiative, an absence of spark about these Eastern Armies. It was not until June 18 that Meade learned that Lee's men had not yet reached Beauregard and, grasping the last embers of opportunity, ordered an all-out attack on the Petersburg line. For some reason – probably that lack of grip again – nothing happened, and while the Union divisions waited for the order to attack, Lee's veterans filed into the Confederate trenches and the chance was gone. On June 20, Grant called off the attacks and the Armies settled down to another siege.

This day, June 20, marked the end of mobile warfare for the Army of the Potomac. From then on, until almost the end of the war ten months later, it would have a static role, here in the lines outside Petersburg. The same thing had happened, with more dire effect, to the Army of Northern Virginia: never again would it march freely where it wished, carrying all before it. This seemed to mean stalemate, though, for Grant's campaign. The terrible casualties of the last six weeks were now fully apparent and no obvious successes had been achieved. Banks had made a hash of the campaign in Texas, Butler was clearly incompetent, Hunter was doing little better than Sigel had done in the Shenandoah, Grant had been obliged to begin a siege at Petersburg, and Sherman was still juggling Hood at Atlanta. Where in any of this were signs of victory? Only with Sherman.

During July and August, Sherman had been extending his lines around Atlanta, strangling the supply lines that supplied the citizens with food, and when the besieging lines were about to close completely, Hood was forced to act. He had command of one of the only two Armies the South still had in the field, and however much he wanted to fight, Hood could not stay in Atlanta and let his Army be destroyed. Before starvation left him no other choice, Hood led his men away to the south, an act that made the fall of Atlanta inevitable. Its fall, on September 4, was a boon to President Lincoln, who was astute in building up this victory into a triumph and let it be known that celebrations would be in order. Bells were rung, gun salutes fired, speeches were made in the Senate and editorials appeared in the Press, all announcing a change in Union fortunes – and so it seemed. Suddenly news of victory came in from everywhere.

There was victory at Mobile, victory at Atlanta, victory even in the Shenandoah Valley, where Phil Sheridan had smashed another Confederate cavalry force under Jubal Early. Victory in the field made victory in the polls inevitable, and this inevitability was capped in October when the Democrats' chosen candidate, General McClellan, refused to stand on a peace-at-any-price ticket. McClellan was keen to wield power and anxious for a political career, but when it came to the crunch, he could not do it. He could not climb onto an electoral platform and declare that all those men who had followed his word and obeyed his orders in battle had died for nothing. His bottom line was a refusal to accept any peace without a prior restoration of the Union. This was not a complete disappointment for the Peace Democrats and Copperheads, as McClellan did not set any terms for the restoration of the Union or address the issue of slavery: if the Confederate States would simply agree to embrace the Union, all would be as before.

But this could not happen. After over three years of war and half a million dead, things could never be as before. And so, on November 8 1864, the people of the United States elected Abraham Lincoln for another term. Lincoln's victory was total; he got most of the soldier vote and 2,203,831 votes to McClellan's 1,797,019, and 212 electoral college votes to McClellan's twenty-one, a victory that ensured that the war would go on to its now inevitable conclusion. That conclusion was already in sight. Sherman and 100,000 men had already left the burning ruins of Atlanta and were on the march through Georgia, Thomas was chasing down Hood and his Army of the Tennessee, and Grant was steadily tightening his noose around the besieged Confederates in Richmond and Petersburg.

CHAPTER TEN

PETERSBURG AND SAVANNAH
1864–1865

Petersburg was a vital strategic point. Through Petersburg ran the rail-roads supplying Richmond and, after the siege began, Lee's Army within Richmond. Unfortunately for the Union, it took some time for the siege lines to close. Smith's failure to take Petersburg in June 1864 helped to prolong the war for another ten months and cost the Army of the Potomac a large number of casualties. However, the long-term strategy remained intact. If the Union Army could take Petersburg, Richmond would be cut off from supply, and Lee's Army had either to come out to fight or surrender. Either way, Richmond would fall. All this was to happen, but not until the spring of 1865; until then the war would go on. Northerners who had perked up after the taking of Atlanta and rejoiced at Lincoln's election in November, or wondered how Sherman was getting on in Georgia, now turned their attention to events at Petersburg. To follow the course of these, it is necessary to go back to the start of the siege in June 1864.

During the three days following the initial assaults by Smith and

Hancock, the attacks on Petersburg continued. None were successful; the Union forces were always either an hour late or a division short and, once again, somehow they never quite managed to push their attacks home. Losses mounted, the attacks were getting nowhere and Grant was right to call them off and order more work with the spade. This decision disgusted the rank and file, who had had enough of digging and knew that, given a little competence among commanders, Petersburg should have fallen at the first attempt. It had, of course, also been touch and go for the Rebel forces, but they had managed to hold on and continued to do so until eventually, on June 18, the Union attacks petered out. Yet another line of trenches sprang up around Petersburg as its besiegers went underground, thus instigating a siege that would last until the final days of the war.

The siege of Petersburg marks an interesting stage in the long history of warfare for it ushered in trench warfare of a kind that was to become terribly familiar in the First World War – and, had it been carefully studied, would have revealed to the Great War generals, beyond any possibility of doubt, that resolute men in trenches, armed with modern weapons, could only be dislodged at great cost. In some respects, this was a strange siege. Petersburg was not totally surrounded and Confederate forces intended to keep it that way by holding the two wings of the Union Army apart as they attempted to encircle the town. For the rest of the summer, the road to Richmond was open and two railroads from the Carolinas still ran into the town. The Union trenches covered only the Bermuda Hundred to the north and the country east of the town, a distance of around five miles south of the Appomattox river. Otherwise the ground was effectively No Man's Land, held by standing and mobile patrols and roving bands of cavalry from either Army.

Over the next few weeks, the task of Grant's Army was to extend the existing trench system into a solid wall and so cut Petersburg off entirely from any possibility of assistance. As the weeks went by, the trenches around Petersburg became ever more elaborate. Siege works were not in themselves sufficient; they kept the Rebels in place yet did little to advance the campaign or give the Union some much-needed successes. Incomplete as it was and so far marked by failure, this move on Petersburg had nonetheless achieved one thing that Lee had been most anxious to avoid; it had driven the Army of Northern Virginia into a defensive position with no way out that did not mean abandoning the Confederate capital. It also left Hood out there in Georgia, with no possibility of support and dwindling sources of military supply. The same was true in Petersburg, where Grant had access to the sea and more reinforcements were arriving all the time. His force would grow stronger, not least with the arrival of Sherman's Army, which would come north when it had finished destroying Georgia and South Carolina, a task which Sherman would begin after taking Atlanta.

Sooner or later therefore, if nothing intervened – and nothing could – Lee, his Army and the Confederacy were doomed. Unless, of course, Lee could break out of the Richmond–Petersburg lines and go rampaging again across the South. To do that, some way had to be found to reduce the growing strength of Grant's Army and lure it away from Petersburg. A diversion might oblige Grant to raise the siege, and such a possibility was enhanced by events in the Shenandoah Valley, where General Hunter was making an indifferent showing against the Confederate forces. The original plan to which Hunter had been supposed to work when sent north to replace Sigel, was for him to link up with Sheridan, clear the Rebels out of the Valley and then march down to join Grant at Petersburg. This scheme came to nothing. When marching on Lynchburg, Hunter had been engaged by a strong Confederate force under Jubal Early; Early drove Hunter out of the Valley into the new Union State of West Virginia, where he stayed motionless for some weeks, licking his wounds.

This gave Early a free hand in the Shenandoah Valley. Ever willing to attack, he turned north and began to march up the Blue Ridge towards the Potomac and Washington, causing a considerable scare among the citizens and assembled politicians who suddenly realised that the nation's capital was virtually undefended. Grant's action in denuding Washington of an abundance of defenders in the spring, when he had combed out all the garrisons to reinforce the field army, was duly criticised, but it was a little late to complain with Confederate infantry marching hard for the capital's suburbs. By July 11, the leading Confederate files were at Silver Springs on the Seventh Street road, almost in sight of the Capitol.

All eyes fell on Halleck, the senior general, to take charge of the garrison, such as it was. Halleck mustered his forces and sent a frantic message to Grant, requesting the immediate despatch of troops. This was most sensible, for those defending Washington were neither numerous nor fit to fight. There was a militia regiment on a ninety-day term of duty, a collection of old men in the Veteran Reserve Corps, willing enough but really best suited to guarding supply lines and depots, a few National Guardsmen, and those gunners from the heavy artillery who had managed to evade Grant's sweep in the previous spring. There were not many of them and they were not very good, but they would have to do until better arrived. Halleck ordered them into trenches and they began to fire away at the fleetingly glimpsed men in grey coming in among the houses.

Early put his men into line of battle and sent them forward while more Union troops, many of them wounded veterans, came limping from the Washington hospitals to pick up a musket and have another crack at Johnny Reb. Even the rear echelon troops were coming into the fray, with more than 1,500 men of the Quartermasters Corps taking up muskets for the first time since their training camps and filing into the Washington trenches. In fact, the situation was critical and might have gone badly for the Union had Early realised how scanty and poor the Union defences actually were. Given one good push, the Union line would have been driven in, but Early could not believe that the Union had left its capital so empty of troops. He came on cautiously and this was a pity for the Confederate cause since it was now mid-July: if the Rebels could drive Lincoln out of his capital, the election results in November would hardly be in his favour.

Eventually, after a day of probing attacks, Early decided that the opposition in front of him was not enough to keep his men from having a high old time in the Union's capital. On July 12, he brought up his artillery and prepared to bombard the city defences before putting in a strong and decisive assault. Unfortunately, he had left it just a little too late. Even as Early's men were flinging out their battle lines and starting forward towards the Capitol, transport steamers from City Point at Petersburg were warping in to the Seventh Street Wharf on the Potomac. Lines were slung ashore, gangplanks fixed and a swarm of tanned soldiers in well-worn Union blue tumbled down onto the jetty and began to form up. The VI Corps, crack troops from the Army of the Potomac, had arrived in the nick of time and now they set out towards the sound of the guns, eager to show these civilians what American infantry could do.

In the event, they did not have to do very much. Their presence was enough to convince Early that the city could not be taken, and after a few hours of skirmishing which Lincoln came out to watch, alarming his men by coming forward to within range of the Rebel muskets, Early withdrew. He returned next day for another tentative probe before retreating towards the Potomac. But he had given the Administration a scare, one which had consequences, for it made Grant realise that a major step in the reduction of the South, and a considerable step towards the reduction of Richmond, required the suppression of all resistance in the Shenandoah Valley.

Here again, Grant demonstrated his strategic grasp on the war. The Shenandoah had long been a thorn in the Union side. Not only did it provide the Confederacy with a great deal of food; it also offered a direct route into the North, towards Maryland and Washington. Nor was this route a two-lane highway, equally open to both sides. The Valley slants north-east to south-west, so Union forces marching south were being taken away from the main spheres of action. With nothing much happening at Petersburg except continual skirmishing, it was time for the Eastern Armies to take the Shenandoah once and for all.

The man Grant had in mind for the task was the Army of the Potomac's cavalry commander, Phil Sheridan, recently returned from wrecking the railroad lines around Richmond. Sheridan was much more than a cavalry officer; he had commanded infantry and was noted as a hard driver, a man who would push the men on and get the job done, regardless of cost. This was to be his task in the Shenandoah from August 1864, when he was ordered by Grant to drive out the Rebels and, 'so devastate the Valley that a crow flying across it would be obliged to carry its own food'. Grant's orders were wide-ranging and gave Sheridan considerable scope to pursue the enemy wherever found, 'following them to the death', but in making this appointment, Grant ran into trouble from Secretary of State Edwin Stanton. Stanton felt that Sheridan was too young and too truculent, or just not the right man for the job, and Stanton ran the War Department and had the ear of the President.

Fortunately for Grant, in spite of the summer's reverses, Lincoln still had faith in the judgement of his chosen commander. If Grant thought Sheridan was the right man for the Shenandoah, Lincoln saw no reason to dispute that decision but, he warned Grant, 'There is no idea of anyone here (in Washington) of following the enemy to the death in any direction. I repeat to you it will neither be done, or attempted, unless you watch it every day, and force it.' Grant took this advice and decided to go directly to the Shenandoah Valley and have it out with Hunter, rather than let the War Department tinker with his instructions. This could have been difficult, for Hunter commanded the Military Department which included the Shenandoah and as such was in charge of everything that happened there. But Hunter was no longer young and had had enough of war; he suggested that Sheridan should take over the entire Department and do as he saw fit, an offer Grant quickly took up.

Meanwhile, matters were proceeding at Petersburg. Grant was slowly extending the siege lines to the west. If he kept on doing that, then sooner or later they would cut the railroads supplying the city, thereby forcing Lee to come out and fight. The problem, as ever, was one of time. It was now August, the casualty lists were long and growing, and the war-weariness of the North was being widely expressed in the newspapers. What was needed, pending some movement from Sherman, still entrenched and facing Hood around Atlanta, was a victory of some kind at Petersburg.

The prospect of some success at Petersburg was not improved on July 30 when an attempt at breaching the Confederate lines by mining failed spectacularly with more terrible losses. Mining has always formed part of siege warfare and in early July the commander of the 48th Pennsylvania, a regiment largely composed of coal miners, suggested to the commander of the IX Corps, Ambrose Burnside, that they could dig a tunnel, 500 feet long and twenty feet deep, under the Confederate trenches to lay a mine and blow the Rebels sky-high. This proposal went up from Burnside to Meade and then to Grant. Neither officer was very keen on this proposal, but no other scheme was in hand to achieve a breach and in the end it was decided that nothing much could be lost by giving the miners a free hand. It took a full month to dig the tunnel and in that time enthusiasm for the project grew. By the time the sappers were ready to blow the charge, this plan had escalated into a full-scale assault; Burnside was ordered to attack with his entire corps immediately after the mine exploded.

Burnside was in command because his corps had dug the tunnel and held that part of the front. He stood no higher in Grant's esteem than before and his plan should have been carefully checked. The IX Corps had four divisions, but three of them were under-strength and very weary. The last, commanded by Brigadier General Edward Ferrero, was completely fresh and contained 4,500 men, 50 per cent more than any of the other divisions, largely because this division had been employed guarding wagon trains well behind the front line. It was therefore logical for Burnside to chose this as his assault division, but there was a snag: Ferrero's division was entirely composed of black soldiers.

There seems no good reason why black troops should not make good soldiers. Quite the contrary. Black recruits, even former slaves, made excellent soldiers and were far easier to handle and better disciplined than the majority of white troops. They were also good fighters. The 54th Massachusetts Regiment of coloured troops, employed in the assault at Battery Wagner outside Charleston in 1863, had pressed home their attack with a skill and valour that had attracted the admiration of the entire Union Army, and other black troops, when given the chance of action, took it eagerly and did well. The snag was that they were not often given the chance, partly for fear of what might happen to any black soldier taken prisoner – many of them were shot out of hand, and the massacre of black soldiers by Bedford Forrest at Fort Pillow had not been forgotten – and partly because of an ingrained feeling that black soldiers were not quite up to the job and lacked the necessary aggression. Perhaps this is one reason why the steam went out of Burnside's planned assault: there was the belief that if black troops were involved, it would not succeed.

Even so, Ferrero's division were given the task of spearheading the assault and the troops pushed forward eagerly with their plans and preparations, keen to show what they could do. The plan continued to expand, with more artillery being brought in to support the attack, and plans were laid not simply to occupy the crater but for an actual breakthrough, a complete penetration into Petersburg. Then finally, at 0445hrs on July 30, after an hour or more of waiting for the mine to go off, eight tons of powder detonated under the Confederate defences. The blast created a vast crater that remains visible more than a hundred years later but the follow-up by Burnside's divisions was lamentable – and far too slow. Ferrero's troops went forward but they were dazed by the noise and when they got into the crater, tumbling down steep walls of soft earth, they were unable to climb out again. The Confederates were able to rush troops forward to line the edge of the hole and the troops trapped below were cut to pieces in the pit. The casualties soared to the thousands and the blame for this catastrophe was laid, correctly, on the IX Corps commander, Ambrose Burnside. He was relieved of his command, but no one had any better ideas for breaching the Confederate defences and so the siege continued into the drenching rains of early autumn and the first chills of winter.

Fortunately, as the autumn arrived, there was better news from other fronts. When the despatch arrived in early September, announcing the fall of Atlanta, Grant celebrated the event with a 500-gun salute, every gun shotted and fired at the Confederate lines. Good news also came in from the Shenandoah Valley, where Jubal Early had finally been caught and defeated by Phil Sheridan. Sheridan thrashed Early at Winchester on September 19 and, more narrowly, at Cedar Creek in mid-October. These smaller successes, capping Sherman's capture of Atlanta at the start of the month, were enough to outweigh the stalemate at Petersburg, and during October majority opinion in the North swung behind Lincoln. It became clear to Grant that, if only something could be done about the Army of Northern Virginia, there was every possibility that the war might be brought to a conclusion by the end of the year.

This belief was underlined by what was happening in Georgia. One week after Lincoln's re-election, William Tecumseh Sherman led his Army out of Atlanta, leaving that city in flames, and set out for the coast of Georgia. Sherman had spent two months in Atlanta, partly to rest his Army, partly in attempts to lure Hood back into battle. The Army enjoyed the rest but Hood declined to co-operate, so in mid-October Sherman sent half his Army – mostly from the Army of the Cumberland – back to Tennessee under 'Pap' Thomas, with orders to keep an eye on Hood, who was always dangerous and on the Tennessee line with some 40,000 men. With that taken care of, Sherman took the rest of his Army, 60,000-strong, and set out to march through Georgia.

Sherman had seen a chance here. His intention was not to defeat a Confederate Army which he could not bring to battle, but rather to demonstrate to the Rebel soldiers and population that the Confederacy was no longer defensible and therefore no longer a viable State. 'If we can march a well-appointed army right through his territory,' he wrote to Grant, 'it is a demonstration to the world, foreign and domestic, that we have a power which Davis cannot resist. This may not be war, but rather statesmanship.' Grant was dubious at first but two factors combined to change his mind. First, he had every faith in Sherman's judgement; if Sherman said this march could be made, he could most probably make it. Secondly, against the argument that Sherman would be cutting himself off from all sources of supply, Grant could recall his own experience in the later stages of the Vicksburg campaign. The South always had an abundance of food; the problem for the Confederacy was not growing crops or breeding cattle, but transportation, moving this food from the fields to the cities or getting it to the armies. This is why both sides were so eager to tear up railway lines and so quick to repair them as they advanced; the criss-crossing continental railroads were the sinews of this war, and if they could be kept cut, the opposing side was at a disadvantage.

For the march through Georgia, Sherman moved his men into four corps columns, split into two commands, one under Otis Howard, one under Henry W. Slocum, with Sherman in overall command, riding somewhere in the centre. The pace of advance was restricted to no more than fifteen miles a day and the Army was surrounded by a screen of cavalry and a crowd of foragers – 'bummers' – whose sole task was to keep the Army fed. The bummers had another task, one in which the rest of Sherman's Army gladly joined: that of leaving a swath of destruction across Georgia – a fate that the other States of the Confederacy would surely share if this war was not rapidly brought to a conclsion.

Georgia therefore burned. Crops, fences, barns, farms, plantations, villages, towns – everything was put to the torch. It was said that Sherman's Army, like that of the ancient Israelites, marked their path with a pillar of fire by night and pillars of smoke by day. Eight days after leaving Atlanta, Sherman's men marched into Milledgeville, then the capital of Georgia, where a small Confederate force was beaten off and the town given to the flames. That was all the resistance encountered other than a certain amount of sniping from the thickets that only led to further destruction of nearby villages and farms. By now, Sherman's

Army had also picked up a great number of fugitive slaves and so, glutted by rich food, surrounded by former slaves willing to do their chores, groom their horses and cook their food – and execrated by the people they despoiled – on December 10 1864, Sherman's men came out on the Georgia coast and turned towards Savannah.

The Confederacy had a garrison of some 12,000 troops at Savannah under General Hardee but they did not stay to be attacked or besieged. General Hardee led his men out of the city and the Union troops marched in, flags flying and bands playing, the men fit, well-fed and triumphant after their devastating march across Georgia. And Sherman's Army had not done yet; Sherman now had it in mind to head north, join up with Grant in Virginia and help finish the war by defeating the Army of Northern Virginia. That path would take the Union men through South Carolina, the first State to secede from the Union and the birthplace of the war. Sherman's men were eager to take their revenge for that act of treachery, and what they would do in South Carolina would make their march through Georgia seem no worse than a gentle progress.

What Sherman had done in Georgia – and would do again to even greater effect in South Carolina – was to demonstrate that the Confederacy could no longer maintain even the first function of a State, the ability to protect its citizens. By the end of the year, the Confederacy was finally coming apart as Grant's strategy began to take effect. With this latest march Sherman had shattered Georgia. Now he was about to destroy South Carolina. In Virginia Sheridan had cut the railroads around Richmond and then taken charge in the Shenandoah Valley. Mobile had gone and the blockade of Southern ports meant that there was no help from outside. Even in Richmond, the Confederacy was seen to be on its last legs, barely able to defend or feed itself.

The only thing that kept the Confederates going was the

unwillingness of Jefferson Davis and Robert E. Lee to concede defeat – and the inability of Grant to break the Confederate lines at Petersburg. Nevertheless, this could only be a matter of time, and with Lincoln re-elected, time was no longer so pressing. Lee's Army was underfed, short of supplies, lacked horses to move its guns and, worst of all, Lee witnessed a steadily sinking morale, evidenced by a flow of deserters into the Union lines, a terrible sign of weakness in this Army famed for its fighting spirit. When Sherman had completed his devastation of Georgia and arrived in support of Grant at Petersburg – as was his intention – those stout defences would be breached and the war would end in an overwhelming Union victory.

One man who was determined to stop that outcome was the feisty Confederate commander in the West, General John B. Hood. After Sherman had driven him away from Atlanta, Hood had taken his Army, some 40,000 seasoned troops, still full of fight, up into the north of Alabama where he had rested his men and horses and gathered supplies. Hood set out from there in late November, apparently preparing to invade Tennessee and take Nashville. This alarmed Washington, which wanted Hood stopped, and the man deputed to stop him was 'Pap' Thomas with his Army of the Cumberland.

Thomas currently had his headquarters in Nashville, where he was rebuilding his command after a considerable portion of it had gone off with Sherman on the march through Georgia. Thomas now had 50,000 men and needed a little more time to bring his forces up to strength; he therefore sent part of his command, two Army corps, some 22,000 men under John Schofield, down to the Tennessee– Alabama border with orders to delay Hood's advance until Thomas was ready to engage him. The move was not entirely wise: Hood outnumbered Schofield and it is not a sound idea for a general to split his force in the presence of the enemy.

This may have been the reason why all the activity around Nashville bothered Grant considerably – or it might have been simply that Grant, who had been continually on active service for almost four years, was now getting tired. Whatever the reason, General Grant was worried and began to badger Thomas with a stream of advice and complaints. There was a chance that Hood could beat Thomas, overrun Tennessee, maybe even get up to the Ohio, but in Thomas's opinion it was a rather slim chance. Like the rest of the Confederate commanders, Hood simply did not have an army big enough for a prolonged campaign, and if he attacked Thomas – well, people had attacked Thomas before and got nowhere.

Perhaps Thomas was unwise to split his force with Hood coming down upon him, but if Hood failed to take advantage of this fleeting opportunity to smash the two parts of Thomas's force separately, it was hardly likely that he could destroy it once they were combined. Hood met Schofield's force at Spring Hill, managing to out-manoeuvre it, marching around the Union Army and getting his troops across Schofield's line of retreat. Then, somehow, Hood's arrangements fell apart and Schofield was able to march his force away, beating off an attack from Nathan Bedford Forrest's cavalry as he went and turning to meet the Confederates again at Franklin on the Harpeth river where the Rebels were eventually obliged to draw off, having lost 6,000 men, including a quantity of generals. That done, Schofield marched his force north and rejoined Thomas at Nashville.

All this should have indicated that there was nothing much to worry about in Tennessee. Nevertheless, Grant did worry. He continued to plague Thomas with advice, orders and exhortations to attack until Thomas told Halleck bluntly that if General Grant had no faith in his ability, he would prefer to resign his command. Grant took him at his word and drafted the order removing Thomas, replacing him with

General John Logan, who was given the order and sent to Nashville to deliver it. Logan was on his way there when word reached him that Thomas had moved out of Nashville and on December 15 had smashed Hood's Army completely. With this demonstration that he knew just what he was doing, Thomas's position was secure, so Logan tore up his orders and returned to Grant's headquarters. Shielded by Nathan Bedford Forrest, Hood withdrew across the Tennessee river but his Army was beyond repair. More than half of his original 40,000 were dead, in captivity or had simply gone home. The only other Army left to the South was the Army of Northern Virginia at Petersburg and now it stood alone. So the New Year of 1865 began – and the Confederacy had just over four months left to live.

CHAPTER ELEVEN

THE ROAD TO APPOMATTOX
January–April 1865

The end of the war might not have been in sight during the bleak January of 1865, yet it was surely coming. The future was still obscured by the winter rains, but when spring came round again the Union Armies would surely move, and when they did so, the fragile fabric that still protected the Confederacy would split apart. Before that, though, there would be more fighting, much of it in the muddy trench lines around Petersburg.

Not that the war ever stopped. Grant was still chipping away at the defences of Petersburg, Sherman, having given Lincoln the city of Savannah as a Christmas present, was readying his men for another great march through the Carolinas to Richmond, and as the New Year came in, Grant sent Ben Butler, who was doing no good anywhere else, to take Fort Fisher, the bastion protecting the last Confederate port at Wilmington in North Carolina. Grant relates how the taking of Fort Fisher and the closing of Wilmington were important, 'not only because it was desirable to cut off their supplies and so ensure the speedy ter- mination of the war, but because foreign governments, particularly the

British Government, were threatening that unless ours could maintain the blockade of the coast, they would cease to recognise any blockade'. At this stage of the war, however, such a claim seems unlikely. Certainly, one of the rules of a maritime blockade is that the blockading power must maintain it and turn ships away: simply telling other nations not to trade with the Confederacy was not enough. But since it was now clear to all that the Confederacy was on its last legs, no nation, let alone Britain, had any interest in prolonging the agony for a day longer than necessary. Grant really sent Butler to take Fort Fisher because he wanted him out of the way.

This task, which only involved taking the seaward defences of Fort Fisher, proved too much even for Butler's modest talents and the task had to be handed over to General A. H. Terry. With a little help from Grant's former naval colleague, the now Rear Admiral David Porter, Terry took Fort Fisher on January 15 1865 and for this exploit he was promoted to brigadier general. This marked the end of Ben Butler's military career. He was the last of the political generals and their time was over. With the election won, four years of clear mandate ahead and the end of the war in sight, Lincoln no longer had any need of Butler's support and was more than ready to respond to a renewed plea from Grant for Butler's dismissal. 'The Wilmington expedition,' Grant wrote to the President, 'has proven a gross and culpable failure ... who is to blame will, I hope, be known.' Butler was promptly retired and went back, grumbling and disgruntled, to his home in Massachusetts. The professional soldiers finally had full control of the war.

The loss of Wilmington was significant in that it increased the South's isolation. No longer could the Confederacy rely on foreign aid in the shape of muskets and ammunition; from now on it had to depend on the inadequate resources of its own arms factories in Richmond – at least until Richmond fell – and on whatever resources its soldiers could glean on the battlefield. Meanwhile the North's resources were growing, technically as well as numerically; over the winter General James H. Wilson was putting together a full corps of mounted troopers, 12,000-strong, all armed with the new repeating carbines, a force that could move fast and produce an amazing amount of firepower – the forerunner of the mounted infantry arm, for Wilson's force would move on horseback but fight on foot.

By the end of January 1865, Sherman was on the move again, his Army of the Tennessee marching north from Savannah into South Carolina, the soldiers fully determined 'to make South Carolina howl'. The rebellion had begun in South Carolina and Sherman and his men had not forgotten just how many good men had been killed in the course of suppressing it. For all those deaths the State would pay a heavy price in burned towns and shattered houses, devastated farms and ruined plantations. The march into South Carolina was entirely Sherman's idea. Grant's original intention was to send transports to Savannah to bring Sherman's troops round by sea to the James river. Sherman was making his preparation to embark when the difficulty in finding sufficient transports led him to suggest that it might be just as well if he marched his Army north through the Carolinas. Grant was happy to accept this proposal, for if North and South Carolina were devastated, yet another source of supply for Lee's Army would be cut off and Lee's resources would depend on a small area of Virginia. Sherman entrenched Savannah so that it could be held by a small Union force and, by the middle of January 1865, he was ready to move north.

The southern countryside was half-waterlogged already and rain fell constantly throughout Sherman's march, though never in sufficient quantities to put out the fires his men started in every building, farm and village. Charleston, where the war had begun with the Confederate guns firing on Fort Sumter, fell without a shot being fired, its supply lines cut by the passage of the Union Army. At Columbia, the State capital, a force of Confederate cavalry put up a brief resistance and then left the town to its fate. The Union troops duly burned their way through the suburbs and into the city centre, leaving the entire city a sea of flame as they marched out the far side.

Nor was Sherman alone in this task of shattering the South. Major-General Edwin Canby was ordered against Mobile, Montgomery and Selma, Alabama, destroying bridges and railroad track on the way. Mobile Bay had been taken earlier but the city itself was still in Confederate hands and Grant wanted the city and the port. Sheridan, in the Shenandoah Valley, was ordered to move on Lynchburg, take it and then move out in every direction, destroying anything of use to the Rebels, from grain stocks to machine shops. In East Tennessee, Major-General George Stoneman was directed to take 4,000 or 5,000 cavalry and devastate the State, and all this while Sherman was eating out the vitals of South Carolina. The aim, Grant stated in a letter to Canby, 'is to leave nothing for the rebellion to stand on'.

Grant was again applying his strategic plan, which broadly consisted of having all his troops in action against the enemy, all the time. This pressure on his subordinate generals seems to have been necessary, but even with it, Grant had great difficulty making his plan work. For some reason – the weather, the state of the roads, an unwillingness to move quickly or take risks – not much happened in Alabama and Tennessee, and a month after sending orders to Canby, Grant was writing to him again, restating his orders in the most direct and unfriendly terms:

> I am in receipt of a despatch informing me that you have made requisitions for a construction corps and material to build seventy miles of railroad. I have given instruction that none

shall be sent … if there had been any idea of repairing railroads, it could have been done much better from the North, where we already had the troops.

I expected your movements to be co-operative with Sherman. This has now entirely failed. I wrote to you long ago, urging you to push promptly and live upon the country and destroy railroads, machine shops etc, not build them. Take Mobile and hold it, and push your forces into the interior, to Selma and Montgomery. Destroy railroads, rolling stock and every thing useful for carrying on the war and when you have done this, take such positions as can be supplied by water. By these means alone you can occupy positions from which the enemy's roads in the interior can be kept broken.

Even with the end of the war in sight, Grant was still pursuing his policy of total war. Whether this was wholly wise remains debatable, for destroying a country that would shortly return to the Union would only increase the bitterness among the local populations and cost the Union a great quantity of money in reconstruction. It may be that Grant was not yet convinced that the end of the war was coming. It may be that he believed it would come quicker if the South was reduced to a desert. It is even possible that he wanted to make the outcome of the rebellion so dreadful that no State would ever again contemplate leaving the Union. The most likely explanation, however, is that total war was the kind of war Grant understood.

Jefferson Davis was now critically short of generals, and although he detested Joe Johnston, he now restored him to the command of all the forces outside Petersburg. This amounted to those in the Carolinas, a total of some 30,000 men. There was little Johnston could do; he had few troops, fewer supplies and no means to take any decisive steps against

Sherman's massive and fast-moving Army of 60,000 men as it blazed a trail across the Carolinas. The march of the Army of the Tennessee across South Carolina was an epic in another sense, for as Joe Johnston was to ruefully remark later, 'I made up my mind that there had been no such army in existence since the days of Julius Caesar.'

Johnston was right. Not simply was there no force available to stop Sherman's Army; this Army was unstoppable. It was an army from the West, from the land of the pioneers, one composed of people who were creating a country out of a wilderness with their bare hands, muscle and sweat; nothing was beyond their capabilities. Whatever was needed, they could create. Bridges were built, roads constructed and forests cleared. This was a winter campaign, one of freezing nights, drenching days and long marches in bitter weather over unmade roads, but the Army of the Tennessee was made up of men to whom hardship was a daily fact of life. They were marching to restore the Union and end this war and nothing was going to stop them. As soldiers, they were indeed worthy descendants of the legions of Rome. Johnston could not stop them and said of Sherman, 'I could do no more than annoy him.'

Desperate situations call for desperate measures and in Richmond the Confederate Congress finally brought itself to do something that they had thought not only impossible but unthinkable: they decided to enlist slaves into the Confederate Army. The idea included acceptance of the fact that the minute a slave entered the army, he would be a free man and could not be returned to slavery later. This in turn led on to another fact: that it would not be possible to free half the slaves and keep the other half in subjection. The war was going to end slavery, one way or another, but not everyone in the Confederate Congress thought it should end like this and there was bitter opposition to the Bill before it was finally endorsed, far too late to make a difference – even if slaves could have been found to fight for their former masters. And to this attempt to raise forces, the Confederate Congress added another attempt to gain foreign recognition. We will free the slaves, Secretary of State Judah Benjamin told Britain and France, in return for aid and recognition. As with most other matters in these dark and final days, it was far too late for that; had the South made such an offer in 1862 after Antietam or in 1863 before Gettysburg, it might have been different, but there was no chance of foreign recognition now.

With this door closed, the South tried to negotiate a peace with the Union Government, sending a delegation north to seek terms from Lincoln. Grant's headquarters that winter were at City Point on the James river, a tent city south of the Bermuda Hundred and just east of Petersburg. City Point was the heart of the great Union supply base that had grown up to support the siege of Petersburg and, as the head-quarters of the Army, the scene of many high-level meetings. On February 3 1865, a delegation from the Confederate Government in Richmond led by Alexander Stephens, Vice-President of the Confederacy, arrived at City Point, mandated to ask Lincoln if there was any way that the two countries could be brought amicably together. This move had been prompted by a suggestion from Frank P. Blair, a man of some influence in the North, who had been to Richmond and suggested to Jefferson Davis that there might be a reunion of the two countries before a joint expedition to drive the French out of Mexico, where Napoleon III was attempting to install one of his surrogates as king in defiance of the Monroe Doctrine. This proposal was entirely Blair's idea, without any help from Lincoln, but it led to the arrival of the Confederate delegation at City Point, where they were courteously received and given comfortable quarters on a river steamer.

Lincoln came to listen to what they had to say but had nothing new to offer. The very phrasing of the Confederate proposal, referring to the 'two countries', was redolent of Southern unreality. To Lincoln and the

North there were never 'two countries'; there was simply one country fighting a rebellion. Lincoln was now dealing from strength and his terms were simple: peace would come when the Confederate Armies laid down their arms and disbanded, and not before. Until then, the war would go on and peace thereafter would involve the restoration of the Union and the abandonment of slavery. This last point was non-negotiable and not just a wish of the President. The Thirteenth Amendment to the Constitution, abolishing slavery in the United States, had already been debated in Congress and submitted to the States for ratification.

Lincoln had no wish to ruin the Southern people; he was even willing to recommend that the slave owners be compensated for the loss of their slaves. Neither had he any wish for vengeance after the war was over. Lincoln was rock-firm for the Union yet willing to offer reasonable terms to bring the Rebels back within it. Slavery must go but the slave holders could be compensated for the loss at the rate of $400 a head. This offer produced a predictable outcry in the North – where the idea of buying men in any form was anathema – but Lincoln could point out that, with the war costing millions of dollars a day, it would be cheaper than more months of fighting and would spare the lives of countless young men. At the end of hostilities, Lincoln proposed, the Southern population would be simply welcomed back into the Union as full citizens. That at least was Lincoln's intention: there were those in the North with a far harsher agenda, politicians and businessmen fully determined to extract reparations from the South, both for starting this war and for the heavy cost of winning it.

The Southern delegates knew this and should have come to terms with the best friend they had, but the meeting at City Point ended in failure; there was no common ground for a settlement and so the war continued. The offer of compensation to the slave holders was never taken up for Jefferson Davis, as adamant for the Confederacy as Lincoln was for the Union, rejected all the President's proposals and called for a continuation of the war. In any event, these negotiations hardly mattered. It was too late for talk; the future of the Confederacy now lay in the hands – and in the Armies – of Ulysses S. Grant.

So the siege of Petersburg went on. So too did the devastation of South Carolina until March 7 1865, when Sherman's force moved across the border into North Carolina and army discipline was instantly restored. Anyone starting fires, said an Army Order, would be shot, the stragglers and 'bummers' must return to their regiments and the foraging patrols would from now on be subject to strict control. These orders were obeyed; in Fayetteville, North Carolina, only the arsenal and a gun factory were burned; everywhere else remained untouched. On arriving in North Carolina, Sherman also acquired more men when he was joined by Major-General Slocum and another 21,000 Union soldiers.

Spring was coming to the South and the weather improved. There was even some solid resistance, the first for weeks, after Joe Johnston had put together the remnants of Hood's Army, the garrison Hardee had pulled out of Savannah and a good number of men from various outposts and garrisons who were not ready to give up the fight just yet. Thus supplied, on March 19 Johnston came in and struck the left flank of Slocum's Corps hard at Bentonville. But Johnston did not have enough men to make any real impression, the right wing of Sherman's Army came up to drive him away and on March 23 Sherman's men entered Goldsboro, at the end of yet another long march. Now the forces of Sherman and Slocum were to head north, join up with Grant near Richmond, crush the Army of Northern Virginia and end the war. All this was certain, and when Sherman's Army set out from Goldsboro, the Confederate States of America had less than a month to live.

The tide of Union power was now in full flood. On March 22,

General James Wilson took his cavalry force across the Tennessee river into the heart of Alabama and destroyed the last Confederate arsenal at Selma. In the Shenandoah Valley, Sheridan was stamping out the last embers of Rebel resistance and driving the rest of Jubal Early's troops out of Waynesboro. Having done that, Sheridan took his troops down to the focal point of the war, Grant's massive Army outside Petersburg, while on the Gulf coast, General Canby finally overran the land defences of Mobile. Everywhere the Confederate position was crumbling and the Rebels knew it, for every night more and more deserters came over into the Union lines. Few arrived on moonlit nights when they could be picked off by their own sentries, but on nights of mist or rain the Union pickets could cheerfully predict 'a good run of Johnnies'.

It was time to put an end to it all and in early March, Lincoln came down from Washington and Sherman came up from North Carolina for a discussion with Grant on how the war might be soon concluded. The President was asking his generals if there were any way, any terms, that could end this war without more bloodshed. Grant and Sherman pointed out that there would be more battles before this war ended and the only way forward was to get on, beat the enemy to his knees and so win the victory.

Lee was equally well aware of these facts. There was just one chance left; if he could get out of Petersburg and join with Joe Johnston, their combined force might be sufficient for one more campaign, one more battle, perhaps one more victory. If he could dash the cup of victory away from Grant and Lincoln's lips, just as they were about to drain it, perhaps that disappointment might lead to some kind of offer, some sort of settlement. To have the war flare up again, just when it seemed to be over, might give the Northern politicians a shock and from that much might follow. It was a very long shot, but there was no other way out except surrender. Lee therefore decided to break out of Petersburg and would do so as soon as the roads were dry enough to support wagons and cannon.

It was now almost four years into the war. Over 500,000 men had died so far and it was clearly time to end it, even if the way to end it meant more losses. Grant, too, was waiting for the rains to stop and the roads to dry for the opposing siege lines around Petersburg were now fifty miles in length, running from the south-east of Petersburg to the north of Richmond. These lines had grown longer over the winter as Grant kept extending his line to the left, always reaching out towards those vital railway tracks, cutting them one by one. This had compelled Lee to extend his defences and by now he had barely enough men to fill them. If Grant could muster a strong force and push it forward hard and fast at any one point, the chances were Lee's line would snap.

Lee had now arrived at the point Grant had been pushing him towards since their forces had collided in the Wilderness the year before. Lee's only hope now was to give up this fruitless defence of Richmond, get out into open country with as many men as he could find, join up with Joe Johnston and make one last stand somewhere in North Carolina. The alternative was to stay in Richmond and starve until Grant's massive forces came tumbling over the defending trenches. These being the options, Lee struck first. His aim was to put together a striking force and attack Grant's centre, breaking through to cut the new military railroad that supplied Grant's Army. If that happened, the left of the Union Army would have to be pulled back to protect City Point and that should enable Lee to march the rest of his Army out of the Petersburg lines and into Virginia. It was a desperate plan but on March 25, he sent a strong force of infantry under General John B. Gordon against a Union strongpoint east of the centre of Petersburg known as Fort Stedman.

Lee and the Army of Northern Virgina had lost none of their aggression and tactical skill, and surprise was complete. Fort Stedman and the

Union front-line position fell and Confederate troops were soon spilling along the trenches on either side and pushing through the second line towards the railroad. If this gap could be widened, the Union Army would be split in two and the Army of Northern Virginia might break out and push down into the Carolinas. For a few hours it all seemed possible. But the Rebels did not break out – not now. The Union troops on the flanks rallied, reinforcements came up to buttress the second line and contain the breach, and Gordon's attack ran out of steam. There was a day-long flurry of close action, with cannon slamming and musketry fire rippling along the line, and then it slowly died out as dusk fell. The Confederate advance had been held, and 5,000 men had been lost in making it – and then the rains came down once more and continued to fall in a solid, grey sheet for the next three days, transforming the ground into a swamp again, filling the trenches with water.

With the failure of the attack on Fort Stedman, it was Grant's turn to strike a blow. Grant had been tapping at the Rebel lines for months, seeking a weak spot, but they were simply too strong, even when thinly held, to permit a successful assault. Therefore Grant had elected to move like a crab, sideways to the west. He hoped that Lee would have to extend his line and thin it out until it finally snapped or – another possibility – that Lee would simply be unable to thin his front any more: Grant could then outflank the Rebels' trenches and oblige them to come out and fight. The winter rains had put a stop to this strategy, but when the rain stopped after the Fort Stedman fight, Grant sent his forces west again.

An attempt to get an infantry force round the Rebel left was brought up short, but Sheridan was now back from the Shenandoah and at the end of March Grant sent him and his cavalry – 12,000 men – through the village of Dinwiddie Court House to take the vital Confederate road and rail junction at Five Forks, south-east of Petersburg. Five Forks was well outside the Rebel lines, and if Sheridan took it, all the remaining Confederate communications would be at risk. Determined to stop this move, Lee sent out George Pickett with an infantry division and every cavalry trooper he could spare, but Sheridan also had infantry – the V Corps, 16,000 men under Major-General Kemble Warren – and on April 1 he drove into Pickett's force and cut it to pieces – and finally got around Lee's flank. By dusk, Pickett's division had been shattered and 5,000 of them were prisoners, the remnants fleeing west and out of the fight.

The hard-driving Sheridan was insistent that the Union victory would not be ended by any failure to follow up the enemy, and it was Warren who caught the full blast of his determination. For some reason, Sheridan decided that he had not done anything to win this engagement and dismissed him abruptly from command of the V Corps. It is hard, though, to see where Warren went wrong. He had brought his corps up, a hard night march from outside Petersburg on bad roads, Sheridan's orders were not a model of clarity, and the Rebel force had been defeated. Sheridan, however, wanted annihilation not merely victory and so Warren was sacked and went to the rear, his career ruined. Major-General Griffin was given command of the V Corps and the advance continued.

The Confederate line was now crumbling. On the following day, April 2, Grant ordered an all-out attack by every gun and every man along the entire fifty-mile trench front around Petersburg and Richmond. The Union troops received this order with gloom; they had been looking at these defences for months and knew how strong they were, and as the troops filed forward for the assault, men were heard telling each other, 'Goodbye, boys, this means death.' Nor was the tremendous bombardment opened on the Rebel lines to soften them up for the attack any comfort either. It went on for hours until the grey light of dawn began to reveal the details of the Rebel positions. Only then did the

Union troops scramble out of their trenches, go forward – and find the Rebel line weak. Weak in number, anyway, if not in spirit. The remaining Rebels still managed to put up a stiff fight, picking off the officers as they came on and greeting the advancing Union lines with a storm of musketry. Numbers will tell, however, and Confederate resistance, if fierce, did not last long; by full daylight the Union troops were over the Rebel defences, herding thousands of prisoners to the rear.

Union pressure was immense all along the front and Lee no longer had the men to resist it. An hour after the assault had begun, General Horatio Wright and his veteran VI Corps found an over-stretched point in the Confederate line and broke through, driving along the trenches to clear out the defenders; it cost the VI Corps 2,000 Union casualties, but by mid-morning the entire Petersburg position had fallen. That night, while Lee took his men out of the town, Grant and his Army occupied Petersburg and the defences of Richmond. Grant, however, did not press on into Richmond and neither did most of his men; the Confederate capital could wait for another day as the aim now was to destroy the last of the resistance in the field and these remaining Rebel soldiers were still full of fight. That morning, an offer had been made to the 5,000 Confederate prisoners taken at Five Forks; if they would swear an oath to the Union and promise to fight no more, they would be released and could go home. Their cause was lost, so why not do so? Fewer than a hundred Confederate soldiers accepted this offer and they left to the jeers of their comrades.

Lee was now in full retreat, heading south and hoping to link up with Joe Johnston and carry on the fight somewhere in the Carolinas. However remote and impossible that aim was with the Confederacy now in ruins, Grant did not intend to let Lee attempt it. The Rebels were marching fast but they had little ammunition and less food, and the Union troops, led by Phil Sheridan, soon began to overhaul them, forcing Lee to turn west. Then Meade caught up with the Confederates at Sayler's Creek and destroyed almost half of Lee's remaining force, taking many half-starved prisoners. The Confederate supply arrangements had completely broken down and Lee's men had not eaten for two days.

The rest of the Rebel Army, down now to 30,000 men, got away in the darkness but they could not go far; they had to wait while foragers went out to find food and supplies. This brief pause only hastened the end but the pursuit continued and the fighting went on until Palm Sunday, April 9 1865. On that day Sheridan, with cavalry and a full infantry corps, finally got across Lee's front near a little village called Appomattox Court House and brought his Army to a halt. The Army of Northern Virginia could do no more. It had run out of everything but courage and was now completely surrounded. Lee tried to force a passage but it was all over and everyone knew it. The firing died out and some time before noon that day General Lee sent an officer under a white flag to the Union Army, asking General Grant for terms.

CHAPTER TWELVE

GRANT AND THE NATURE OF HIGH COMMAND 1861–1865

Grant had been seeking the surrender of the Army of Northern Virginia for two days before Lee agreed to talks. On April 7, he had sent a letter to his opponent, pointing out that the events of the past week should have convinced him of the hopelessness of the struggle and asking him to prevent 'a further effusion of blood' and to surrender 'that portion of the Confederate States Army known as the Army of Northern Virginia'. Lee replied later that day and, while rejecting Grant's view regarding the hopelessness of the Rebel situation, he agreed on the need to avoid further bloodshed and asked what terms were available on condition of surrender.

Grant had moved on from his Fort Donelson days. In the present situation there was no need for blunt demands for unconditional surrender; if Lee gave in, the war was over. Grant therefore replied on April 8, stating that, 'peace being my great desire, there is but one condition I would insist upon, namely that the men and officers surrendered shall be disqualified from taking up arms against the Government of the United States until properly exchanged'. Grant also offered to meet Lee or any officers Lee designated, for a full discussion of surrender terms.

Grant knew that Lee's hopes were at an end because Union cavalry under George Armstrong Custer had got to the railroad at Appomattox Station and captured the last Confederate supply train. When the head of Lee's columns came down on Appomattox Station on April 9, they found Custer in possession and their much-needed supplies gone. Pointing out the inevitable, early that morning Grant wrote again to Lee, suggesting that if the South laid down its arms, thousands of lives would be saved. At mid-morning – 11.50 am – a letter was received from Lee requesting an interview to discuss terms and the two men met later that day in Mr Wilmer McLean's house in the village of Appomattox Court House.

There was a certain irony in this choice of meeting place. Before the war, McLean had owned a house at Manassas and in April 1861 he found his home an epicentre for the first of the Civil War battles. Vowing to keep well away from the conflict in the future, he sold up and moved south to Appomattox Court House where, four years later, after he had listened anxiously to the sound of approaching battle, he found a group of Union and Confederate officers standing on his porch, asking if they could use his parlour to discuss a peace.

The meeting began awkwardly. Lee arrived in an immaculate uniform, complete with sword, while Grant came in dressed as usual, no sword or other side-arms, just the plain uniform of a Union private with his general's stars tacked on his shoulders. Grant records that his feelings, which had been jubilant on receiving Lee's letter, were now sad and depressed. The elation of victory having worn off, Grant was now thinking of the cost of bringing Lee to this meeting, a cost paid in hundreds of thousands of young American lives. Nor was he happy at the downfall of a gallant opponent, but after an exchange of pleasantries the two men got down to business. The terms were those offered by Grant previously: the Confederate soldiers must give individual paroles not to take up arms and surrender all weapons except the officers' side-arms – and that was it. When these paroles had been received, the men were free to go to their own homes and would not be further disturbed provided they kept their word.

Lee then explained that the men in the Southern Armies owned their own horses and would need these horses to plough their fields for the coming summer. Grant declined to amend the surrender terms but issued an instruction that any man claiming a horse should be allowed to keep it. He also enquired if he could do anything to help Lee's soldiers and, finding out that they were starving, ordered the immediate issue of 25,000 rations to the Confederate troops.

News of the surrender quickly leaked out and was at first greeted in the Union lines with cheering and the firing of a hundred-gun salute, but Grant quickly sent out an order stopping all celebrations. The Confederates were now his prisoners and would soon be fellow citizens again, and he did not want the Union Army rejoicing in their downfall. Grant then set out to carry the news to Washington, while the soldiers in the two Armies put their weapons aside and began to fraternise.

The final act of the drama took place three days later, on April 12, with the formal surrender of weapons by the Army of Northern Virginia. Brigadier General Joshua Chamberlain of V Corps, the man who had held Little Round Top at Gettysburg, had been deputed to accept this surrender and Chamberlain had his men out early, lining the road down which the Confederates would march. The Confederates took their time breaking camp, but when they came out, they did so in style, one long column in grey, bayonets fixed, drums beating and colours displayed. It was a display of pride rather than defiance. This, after all, was no mean army. It was the Army of Northern Virginia, or what was left of it, the Army of Antietam, Fredricksburg, Charlottesville, Gettysburg, the Wilderness and a hundred other fights – an Army that had fought the Union until it could fight no more. This being so, as the head of the Confederate column grew near, Chamberlain ordered his men to the salute, a last soldierly mark of respect before the Army of Northern Virginia halted, stacked its weapons and marched into history.

The war was not quite over. It took time for the word to spread and in the south Joe Johnston was still in arms. Jefferson Davis took his Cabinet papers and fled from Richmond, trying to meet up with Johnston, and he stayed at liberty for a few weeks until captured by Union cavalry in early May. Selby entered Mobile a few days after Appomattox and on April 17 Sherman and Johnston met to agree terms at Raleigh in North Carolina. And so, slowly, over two weeks, the War of the Rebellion petered out. It did not, of course, end without one final tragedy. On April 14, John Wilkes Booth, an actor, shot Abraham Lincoln dead at Ford's Theatre in Washington and Andrew Johnson, the Vice-President of the United States, succeeded to the Presidency.

Lincoln's assassination had some dire long-term effects, not least in ensuring far harsher treatment for the South in the years of reconstruction. Lincoln had only wanted the war over, the Union restored, a rapid return to normality and the end of slavery. Slavery ended for the Negro but freedom was all the blacks obtained, for segregation – 'Jim Crow' – arrived to replace it and America's black population had to wait another hundred years before they gained the rights for which Union soldiers, both black and white, thought they had been fighting in the Civil War.

Sherman was the first to feel the difference in Washington. At their surrender talks, Sherman and Johnston had agreed to terms that were all-embracing; they would dissolve all the remaining Confederate forces, return the Confederate soldiers to civilian life and restore the Union. This was Johnston's idea and when the terms were agreed, he had the Confederate Secretary of State for War, John C. Breckenridge, ratify them on behalf of the Confederacy. Sherman duly signed on behalf of the Union, putting his name to a document which was virtually a peace treaty and thereby restoring the Confederate States to the Union without further ado. Although this was well beyond Sherman's authority – as Sherman himself was well aware – Lincoln might have gone along with it, for he had no desire to persecute the South after hostilities had ceased. Not so Andrew Johnson and the new Administration. They rejected the terms of Sherman's agreement and ordered Grant to go to North Carolina and offer no better terms than those he had offered to Lee. The Southern States had harsh times ahead before they got back into the Union.

At least the war was over. Jefferson Davis was captured on May 10 and Kirby Smith surrendered the last Confederate force on May 26. Even before that, the vast volunteer armies of the Union had started to dissolve, taking their final bow at a two-day review in Washington on May 23 and 24 1865. The first day saw the Army of the Potomac march past, regiment by regiment, infantry, cavalry, artillery and supply wagons, all sparkling from days of spit and polish – the Army of the Potomac always knew how to put on show. On the second day it was the Western Armies which came marching past, the Army of the Cumberland, the Army of the Ohio, and the far-ranging Army of the Tennessee, long columns of infantry who had somehow, in the last few days, learned how to march in step and keep in line. Even those soldiers of the Army of the Potomac who came to see the Western troops go by had to allow that, when they put their minds to it, these fellows also knew how to put on a show.

And then, quite suddenly, it was all over. Grant was there in the reviewing stand with the President and the other generals and representatives of the great and the good, proud to see his soldiers go by, but one face was missing. Lincoln should have been there also; this was really his victory, the outcome of all his work, and he should have had a chance to see it come to fruition. As it was, Grant remained as head of the Army for the next two years. He devoted himself to disbanding the volunteer regiments and reducing the size of the Regular Army to something approaching its pre-war level. Not entirely though – the United States had expanded in the last four years and a larger Army than before would be needed, to conquer and police the Western frontier. In 1868, Johnson completed his term as President and Grant was nominated as his successor and duly elected.

Grant served two terms as President of the United States but his Administration was marked by failure and corruption. Grant himself was not guilty of corruption but he failed to deal with it, either in Washington or in those charged with reconstructing the Union in the Southern States. He also failed to deliver the promises of reconstruction to the former slaves and to halt carpet-bagging and segregation spreading in the South. When he left political office in 1876, he was once again regarded as a failure.

After leaving the White House, Grant and his wife Julia spent the next two years roving the world. Grant was feted everywhere, hailed as a great general, a former President and a fine example of all that America stood for. Dinners and receptions, those events which Grant had once dreaded, became daily events – he even dined with the officers of the Gibraltar garrison in a dining room dug deep inside the Rock – but whether Grant enjoyed all this cannot be known, for he kept no journal.

What can be said, though, is that when this world tour was over, Grant was yet again faced with the problem of earning a living and no real idea of how to go about it. Grant sought a third term as President, but although he attended the Republican Convention in 1880, he failed to get the nomination; his star had faded. He therefore went to New York and applied himself to business, but Grant was no businessman and his ventures after the war were no more successful than those before it. He tried being president of a railroad company, but the railroad in question was in Mexico and never got built. He tried becoming a stockbroker, but the business failed in 1884 and Grant's partner, Fernando Ward, fled abroad, chased by accusations of fraud.

Now in his sixties, Grant was broke – and ill. Cancer had set in and Grant faced the prospect of dying, leaving his much-loved Julia with nothing to live on. A loan from William Vanderbilt staved off his creditors for a while and then help arrived in the shape of a proposal from Century Publishing in New York, that General U. S. Grant should write his memoirs. Negotiating the contract took a little while, with Grant taking a lot of sensible advice from his good friend Samuel Clemens – better known as Mark Twain, author of *Tom Sawyer* and *Huckleberry Finn*. When Century failed to produce an acceptable offer, Clemens proposed a deal which was based on a small advance and substantial royalties after publication. Grant duly wrote the two-volume book and it sold so well that after his death Julia received something in the region of half a million dollars, a fabulous sum in the 1880s, to restore the family fortunes. Writing his memoirs, which appeared in 1885–86, took Grant the rest of his life. He was still at work on them a month before his death, on June 27 1885.

Grant could write. There were suggestions that Clemens wrote most of the book, but he denied this and Grant's voice can be heard in every line. The books were written in longhand, on pads of lined paper, and apart from the research in the Washington archives by his son Frederick, they are entirely Grant's work. Although most of the material is devoted to the war and some incidents, such as the reasons for his resignation from the pre-war Army, are glossed over, it is nevertheless a full account of a remarkable life.

There remains the paradox in Grant's story: how could a man who was so successful in war be such a failure at practically everything else? But this is not the complete picture, for Grant the soldier and Grant the civilian are the same man. Grant must also be remembered as a good husband and father, a good friend, a man who was kind to others in adversity and free from any hint of either jealousy or vindictiveness – in many respects a fine, even a noble, human being. Grant, in short, is an enigma, but as a soldier he shone brightly and it is in that role he has to be assessed here.

A great commander must have courage. Courage is the prince of military virtues, for nothing can be done without it. War is a dangerous game and no place for faint-hearts, yet there are various kinds of courage and physical courage is not necessarily the most important at all times. Civil War generals certainly had to have physical courage; their men expected it and had little time for an officer who would not readily expose himself to danger. As a result, general officers on either side were killed and wounded in great numbers: Longstreet, Hood, Sedgwick, Hancock, Stonewall Jackson, McPherson, Jeb Stuart – the list is virtually endless and the number of general officers killed or wounded on both sides is a tribute to their physical courage. Whether it says much for their common sense is another matter; a general is supposed to use his brains, stay out of the ruck and fight his command totally. A general who lets himself be drawn forward into the battle is no more use to his soldiers than any other soldier and not fulfilling his main purpose.

Another necessity, and a more useful virtue for generals, is moral courage, the ability to take hard decisions and stick to them in spite of all pressures. Not the least of these, and perhaps the hardest, is the courage to send men into battle while staying out of it oneself, knowing that, whatever the outcome, a considerable number of these men are going to be killed. Grant had both physical and moral courage in abundance, and the latter quality was never better displayed than when he ordered the Union Army to march south after that terrible pounding in the Wilderness. It has been said that Grant's decision to march south out of the Wilderness turned the fortunes of the war and led to the Union victory eleven months later. It also led to a summer-long battle of attrition from the Wilderness to Petersburg, but the mounting casualty lists did not deter Grant from his purpose. He knew that, when it came right down to it, the Confederacy 'did not have Army enough' to maintain this war if he could bring the full force of the North against it.

Grant had no need to fight a war of manoeuvre like Lee but he was far more than a master of attrition. He is frequently described as such but while many authorities worship generals of manoeuvre, they forget that a general can manoeuvre for an entire campaign, but unless the enemy gives in without a fight, sooner or later he must be brought to battle. Grant knew this and he knew how to fight as well as manoeuvre. The North had all the power needed to win if only it could find a general who knew how to apply that power. Grant saw that he must use this force to pin Lee in position and fight him to a standstill. He also knew that he had the force to do this, to maintain a battle of attrition if need be, because he could afford to lose men in quantity and Lee could not. There was not much skill here but to make that decision and stick to it took courage.

Grant was lucky in that he enjoyed the support of Lincoln. In June 1864, as the Armies brawled their way across towards Petersburg, the President wrote, 'My previous high estimate of General Grant has been maintained and heightened by the remarkable campaign he is now conducting. He and his brave soldiers are now in the midst of their term of great trial.' Grant's luck was apparent in other ways. He was lucky that, although he had as much experience as any other soldier, he was not too old when the call to arms came. Grant was born in April 1822 and was therefore exactly thirty-nine years old, still a young man, when war broke out. This youth and vitality proved useful. Without them, it is hard to see how he could have withstood the strain of four years' continuous command, with ever-rising responsibility and relentless campaigning. War is a game for young men, with strong constitutions and flexible minds, and Grant was fortunate that war found him when it did.

Grant was fortunate, too, in his subordinates – and he knew it. He was well aware that much of his success was due to the skill and tenacity and generalship displayed by McPherson, Sheridan, Meade and, above all, Sherman. Yet this too is to Grant's credit and is another of the assets needed by a great commander, the ability to select competent subordinate field commanders. A commander cannot do it all himself and many a military leader has seen plans come to nothing because his subordinates were unreliable at the crunch. Grant could rely in these men because they knew their trade. They could also be relied on to obey his orders and execute his plans without demur. In return, Grant stood by them. Lincoln thought that Sheridan was too slight to command the cavalry corps of the Army of the Potomac, but Grant assured him that Sheridan was the right man for the job, as indeed he was.

As for Sherman, he was Grant's rock, his most dependable and imaginative commander. And yet Sherman, too, was a paradox. Although the most ruthless of generals – 'War is hell,' he once declared, 'and I intend to fight it that way' – no one was more willing to help the South once the surrender came, and his treaty with Johnston which got him into so much trouble is evidence of that. Grant depended on Sherman and trusted him absolutely, but here again there is a paradox, for Sherman was unstable. He had had a complete nervous breakdown early in the war and there was a time when the general opinion in the Army thought him mad – and Sherman himself was by no means certain of his own sanity. When Halleck relieved him of his command in Kentucky in 1861, Sherman wrote to his brother, the US Senator John Sherman, 'I am so sensible of my disgrace . . . that I do think I would have committed suicide were it not for my children. I do not think I can ever again be entrusted with command.' But Sherman recovered and returned to the war and was there with Grant until the end. Grant therefore deserves credit for choosing these men and standing by them in adversity; they in turn repaid his trust with good service and great loyalty.

In the campaign of 1864, Grant displayed another necessary, even essential, quality for top command, a professional one – the ability to select the aim and maintain it. Grant had always been able to do this: at every level of command, he never forgot what he was trying to do. He always displayed a grasp of strategy, even as a corps commander, and was always looking ahead to the next move; rather like a chess player, he was determined that every move, every engagement, should contribute to some overall aim. The ability to select the aim may be a professional one but it has to be based on personal qualities, a grasp of priorities, a kind of vision, and this vision has to be all-embracing. It is necessary for a general to know what the long term aim is, but he must also have a sense of priority – not just knowing what the priority is but also knowing what the priority is *now*. A small but useful example of this was at Shiloh. When Grant got off his steamer, chaos was reigning and panic widespread but he had heard that roar of musketry and knew that the first priority was to get more ammunition forward to the front-line regiments; if the ammunition ran out, his position would fall, no matter what arrangements were made to sustain it.

Another quality required by a great commander is common sense, one that is nowhere near as common as it should be among generals.

All the great leaders have it; those without it usually fail. Wellington had it and it enabled him to defeat Napoleon and his marshals whenever they came against him. The basic requirement of common sense in war is in estimating the limits of the possible, in gauging exactly what can be done with the force available and when one is going too far. Common sense can be encapsulated in military instructions but these are, as all good soldiers know, 'for the obedience of fools and the guidance of wise men'. The trick is to know when to abandon the rules and when to follow them and that takes common sense.

Common sense Grant had in abundance and he showed it in his handling of the Vicksburg campaign when, slowly and shrewdly, he saw that there was only one way to take the town and that to do so various prior arrangements had to be made. He displayed it again when he realised that his men could live on what they could forage and without the apparent necessity – and impossibility – of a long supply train.

High command needs experience of command at all levels, from junior officer upwards, service with the fighting units and on the staff. There is no other way to experience the practical limits of the possible. Grant never served on the staff but as commissionary officer for his regiment in the Mexican War he had seen how difficult staff work was, how hard even the simplest task could be when it had to be carried out in enemy territory with inadequate information and resources. Grant had a good, loyal staff in the Civil War and he worked them hard; his orders are a model of clarity and his intentions could not be misinterpreted.

It is noticeable that Grant was a competent officer at every level, attracting commendations in the Mexican War and rising steadily in the Civil War in spite of the nagging opposition of Halleck. Grant knew his business and kept on doing his best, training his troops, ensuring his communications and sources of supply, fighting the enemy wherever found, until somebody noticed how good he was. When Grant was in charge, people noticed the difference, right down to the lowest private soldier, as evidenced by the changes to the Army of the Potomac in 1864, after Grant arrived at Brandy Station and got alongside Meade.

As for his drinking, it is strange how that accusation hung around his reputation, partly because there was little evidence to support the allegations that he was back on the bottle, and partly because in that hard-drinking Army, which had more than its fair share of drunks, Grant might just as easily have been considered abstemious.

Grant was not always successful. Belmont was usually considered as one of his defeats and Shiloh was very close to a disaster, one probably caused by Grant's underestimation of the enemy forces – a mistake he was not to make again. Nor was he correct to say, outside Cold Harbor in 1864, that he would 'fight it out along this line if it takes all summer'. Within days of making that claim, Grant had left his siege lines and ordered the Army over the James and on to Petersburg, where they stayed until almost the end of the war. These reverses and changes of plan are inevitable and should not be allowed to upset the fair judgement on Grant, that he was a very good general and perhaps a great one, the difference between the two residing in the view one takes about Grant's ability to grip.

Grip is one of the intangible military virtues. Soldiers notice it when it is around and when it is lacking, so their commander must have grip. Grip is another word for firm, sensible control but, as with so many words diverted to military uses, it means rather more than that. A general must grip his forces; he must train them, order them, inspire them, make them believe in themselves – and in him. If he can do that, his army will feel his grip.

He must also grip the enemy; he must be able to impose his will on them, be able to outwit their plans and, when it comes to it, outfight their forces. Such a general is unbeatable because he has command of the battlefield and can do what he wants on it. And finally, a great commander must be willing to fight. This necessity was summed up during the Civil War by Grant's West Point mentor, General C. F. Smith, in some advice Smith gave to Lew Wallace:

Battle is the ultimate to which the whole life's labour of an officer should be directed. He may live to the age of retirement without seeing a battle; still he must always be getting ready for it exactly as if he knew the hour of the day it is to break upon him. And then, whether it come early or late, he must be willing to fight – he *must* fight.

Grant was always willing to fight. In Mexico he made his way forward from the safety of the supply train to get into the action, and from the moment he entered the Civil War, he always headed for the sound of the guns. More than that, as he rose in rank, he saw to it that the troops under his command were also in the fight, most memorably by pointing out to the garrison troops in the West in 1864 that they could guard and protect the Union lines just as easily by advancing as by staying put – and strain the enemy's resources at the same time. All this adds up to another virtue, usually called character; Grant had character in abundance and it made up for any lack of that fleeting asset charisma, of which he had none at all.

Grant's legacy to the United States Army was the understanding that wars are fought to be won, that the soldier who was not in action was not at his post, that the aim of a general was to fight all the time, all along the line, regardless of cost, until the enemy gave way and the battle was over. Whether the lessons of 1864 were as applicable in later wars as they were at the time is debatable, but that was Grant's gift to his successors – generals such as Pershing and Eisenhower – and they made good use of it when their time came.

So, was Grant a great commander? The evidence surely supports a claim to that distinction, but the final word might go to General Horace Porter, who served on Grant's staff from the time of Chattanooga. Writing on Grant at the end of the war, Porter says:

> General Grant now stood in the forefront of the world's greatest captains. Most of the conspicuous soldiers in history have risen to prominence by gradual steps but the Union commander came before the people with a sudden bound. Almost the first sight they caught of him was at Donelson. From that event to Appomattox he was the leader whose name was the harbinger of victory. He was the most aggressive fighter . . . he took no backward steps. He possessed in a striking degree every characteristic of the successful soldier. His methods were all stamped with tenacity of purpose, originality and ingenuity. He was never betrayed by success into boasting of his battles. He never under-rated himself in battle; he never overrated himself in a report.

Porter's eulogy goes on for pages and is full of detailed praise for his old commander but it also includes a quote from one of Grant's most persistent opponents, the Confederate General James Longstreet, which seems to sum Grant up, both as a soldier and a man: 'General Grant had come to be known as an all-round fighter, seldom, if ever, surpassed; but the biggest part of him was his heart.' Anyone who knows anything about Ulysses Simpson Grant would certainly agree.

CHRONOLOGY

April 27 1822 Grant born at Point Pleasant, Ohio, eldest son of Jesse and Hannah Grant.

May 29 1839 enters the US Military Academy, West Point, New York

June 1843 graduates from the Academy, 156th in a class of 233.

July 28 1843 gazetted 2nd Lieutenant, 4th Infantry Regiment.

September 20 1843 joins his regiment in St Louis.

October 1843 meets Julia Dent, sister of another officer.

May 1845 becomes engaged to Julia Dent.

June 1845 departs for the war with Mexico.

March 1846 war with Mexico begins.

March 11 1846 Lt U.S. Grant placed in charge of the commissary (regimental supplies).

April 26 1846 first engagement of the Mexican War.

May 7 1846 Grant takes part in the Battle of Palo Alto – Matamoros.

May 1846 Grant takes part in fighting on the Rio Grande.

July 1846 the invasion of Mexico begins. Grant applies for regimental duty, away from the commissary.

September 1846 Battle of Monteray. Grant charges with his regiment.

March 1847 the expedition to Vera Cruz.

March 29 1847 Vera Cruz surrenders.

April 8 1847 the march on Mexico City begins.

September 1847 Grant takes part in the battle of Chapultepec, Mexico City. The Mexican War ends.
Grant awarded two brevet ranks, promotion to 1st Lieutenant and Acting Captain, plus citations for gallant conduct.

August 22 1848 Grant marries Julia Dent.

November 17 1848 Captain and Mrs Grant rejoin the 4th Infantry at Detroit, Michigan.

May 30 1850 the Grants' first child, Fredrick (Fred) born.

June 1852 Grant posted to the Pacific Coast, without his wife.

September 1852 arrives Fort Vancouver, Oregon.

April 1854 Grant resigns his commission after allegations of drunkenness.

1854–1861 Grant tries farming, forestry, and retailing to support his family, with no significant success. Works in his father's store in Galena, Illinois; Grant 'a poor businessman'.

April 15 1861 Fort Sumter falls to Confederate gunfire; the US Civil War begins. Grant decides to return to the Army.
Captain U.S. Grant nominated by Galena citizens to command a locally raised company of Volunteers for the North.

May 4 1861 Grant appointed 'Colonel' and commander of Camp Yates, a training camp at Springfield, Illinois.

May 24 1861 Grant applies to Washington for command of a Union regiment.

June 16 1861 hearing nothing from Washington, Grant accepts post as Colonel in an Illinois volunteer regiment, the 21st Illinois Volunteers.

July 1861 the 21st Illinois march into Missouri.

August 1861 word from Washington: President Lincoln appoints Grant as a Brigadier-General. Reports for duty at St Louis, Mo. Appointed commander in South-East Missouri. Moves headquarters to Cairo.

November 7 1861 defeats a Confederate force at Belmont.

February 1862 Grant lays siege to Forts Henry and Donaldson; insists on an unconditional surrender of the Rebel garrisons. Becomes famous in the north as U.S. (for Unconditional Surrender) Grant.

April 6 1862 Grant, now a Major-General, wins narrow victory at Shiloh.

January 13 1863 Grant assumes command of expedition to seize the Mississippi town of Vicksburg.

July 3 1863 Vicksburg surrenders. Confederacy cut in half.

September 19–20 1863 Battle of Chickamauga a near defeat; Grant sent to Chattanooga to take command of Union Armies west of the Allegheny Mountains and retrieve situation.

November 24–25 1863 Grant wins battle of Lookout Mountain (Chattanooga). Confederates withdraw into Georgia.

March 9 1864 Grant raised to rank of Lt General and appointed General in Chief of all Union Armies.

May 4 1864 Grant's strategic plan starts to evolve; the Army of the Potomac advances into the Wilderness and Sherman moves on Atlanta, Georgia.

May 4–7 1864 Battle of the Wilderness, Virginia.

May 8 1864 unwilling to accept a reverse, Grant orders Army of Potomac to move south to Spotsylvania.

May 8–19 1864 Battle of Spotsylvania, a battle of attrition.

June 3 1864 Grant attacks Lee at Cold Harbor and sustains heavy losses; Union casualties in first month exceed 60,000 men.

June 13 1864 rival armies arrive at Petersburg and Richmond; siege begins.

September 2 1864 Sherman takes Atlanta.

October 1864–April 1865 siege of Petersburg and Richmond continues.

April 1 1865 Lee leaves Richmond and is defeated at Battle of Five Forks.

April 9 1865 Lee surrenders to Grant at Appomattox; end of US Civil War.

April 14 1865 President Lincoln assassinated in Ford's Theatre, Washington.

1865–1869 Grant head of US Army.

November 1869 elected 18th President of the USA; serves until 1877.

July 23 1885 Grant dies at Mount McGregor, New York; buried in Grant's Tomb, New York City.

BIBLIOGRAPHY

An indispensable aid for any student of the US Civil War is the *War of the Rebellion; A Compilation of Official Records of the Union and Confederate Armies*, now available on CD-ROM from The Guild Press of Indiana, Inc, 435 Gradle Drive, Carmel, ID 46032, tel: 317 848 6421, www.guildpress.com, or from Guidon Books, 7117 Main St, Scottsdale, Arizona, 85251, tel: 480 945 8811, www. guidon.com.

Arnold, James, R., *The Armies of U. S. Grant*, Arms and Armour Press, 1995.

Bailey, Ronald and the Editors of Time Life, *The Civil War*; six vols. Time Life, 1985.

Catton, Bruce, *The Civil War*, Houghton Mifflin, 1987.

Catton, Bruce, *This Hallowed Ground*, Doubleday, 1956.

Catton, Bruce, *Mr Lincoln's Army*, Doubleday, 1951.

Catton, Bruce, *Glory Road*, Doubleday, 1952.

Catton, Bruce, *A Stillness at Appomattox*, Doubleday, 1953.

Catton, Bruce, *Grant Moves South*, J. M. Dent, 1970.

Catton, Bruce, *Grant Takes Command*, J. M. Dent, 1970.

Davis, William C., *A Concise History of The Civil War*, National Parks Civil War Series, 1994.

Farmer, Alan, *The American Civil War, 1861-1865*, Hodder and Stoughton, 1996.

Gleason, Michael P., *Civil War Sites*, Insiders' Publishing, Gettysburg, Penns., 1997.

Grant, General U. S., *The Personal Memoirs of U. S. Grant* (two volumes) Charles L. Webster, 1885.

Henderson, George, F. R., *Stonewall Jackson and the American Civil War*, Peter Smith, Massachusetts, 1968.

Howard, Blair, *Battlefields of the Civil War*, Hunter Publishing, Edison, N.J., 1995.

Lewis, Lloyd, *Captain Sam Grant; 1822-1861*, Little, Brown, 1950.

Porter, General Horace, LL. D., *Campaigning with Grant*, Blue and Grey Press, 1984.

Randall, J. G. & Richard, N. Current, *Lincoln the President*, Eyre and Spottiswoode, 1955.

INDEX